10 Rules to Survive the Dating Jungle

1st Book in The Dating Jungle Series

BY TARA RICHTER

Copyright © 2012 Tara Richter

All rights reserved. In accordance with U.S. Copyright Act of 1976, the scanning, uploading, and electronic sharing of any part of this book without permission of the publisher constitute unlawful piracy and theft of the author's intellectual property. No part of this book may be reproduced in any form by any electronic or mechanical means (including photocopying, recording or information storage and retrieval) without permission in writing from the author or publisher. Thank you for your support of the author's rights. If you would like to purchase bulk or wholesale copies, please contact the publisher at richterpublishing@icloud.com.

Published by Richter Publishing LLC
www.richterpublishing.com

Book Cover Design: Richter Publishing

Editors: Casey Cavanagh

Book Formatting: Monica San Nicolas

ISBN-10: 0692623485

ISBN-13: 978-0692623480

LCCN Permalink: https://lccn.loc.gov/2017900087

LCCN 2017900087

Library of Congress Copyright Registration #TX 8-167-275

DISCLAIMER

This book is designed to provide information on dating only. This information is provided and sold with the knowledge that the publisher and author do not offer any legal or medical advice. In the case of a need for any such expertise consult with the appropriate professional. This book does not contain all information available on the subject. This book has not been created to be specific to any individual people or organizations' situation or needs. Reasonable efforts have been made to make this book as accurate as possible. However, there may be typographical and or content errors. Therefore, this book should serve only as a general guide and not as the ultimate source of subject information. This book contains information that might be dated or erroneous and is intended only to educate and entertain. The author and publisher shall have no liability or responsibility to any person or entity regarding any loss or damage incurred, or alleged to have incurred, directly or indirectly, by the information contained in this book or as a result of anyone acting or failing to act upon the information in this book. You hereby agree never to sue and to hold the author and publisher harmless from any and all claims arising out of the information contained in this book. You hereby agree to be bound by this disclaimer, covenant not to sue and release. You may return this book within the guarantee time period for a full refund. In the interest of full disclosure, this book contains affiliate links that might pay the author or publisher a commission upon any purchase from the company. While the author and publisher take no responsibility for any virus or technical issues that could be caused by such kinks, the business practices of these companies and or the performance of any product or service, the author or publisher has used the product or service and makes a recommendation in good faith based on that experience. All characters appearing in this work are fictitious. Any resemblance to real persons, living or dead is purely coincidental.

DEDICATION

I dedicate this book to all of my bad romances. Without you, this book wouldn't have been possible. My girlfriends always said I had a knack for meeting the most interesting people (interesting is a nice way of saying crazy) and they are right. Though, I wouldn't change any of my past relationships for the world. They make for great stories and lessons learned. The world would be so boring if there were only vanilla people in your life. I'd rather have some Rocky Road one day and maybe Neapolitan the next. Yes, some broke my heart and others healed it. But all in all I thank you, every last crazy one of you.

CONTENTS

INTRODUCTION 1

RULE #1 HEAL ALL YOUR WOUNDS FIRST BEFORE LOVING ANOTHER 4

RULE #2 DON'T DATE ANYONE WHO IS MARRIED 23

RULE #3 3 STRIKES YOU'RE OUT 40

RULE #4 AVOID THE KNIGHT IN SHINING ARMOR 51

RULE #5 LOST PUPPY SYNDROME 59

RULE #6 RESPECT YOURSELF & YOUR BOUNDARIES ... 66

RULE #7 STEER CLEAR OF ADDICTS 75

RULE #8 HAVE FUN, BE YOURSELF & DON'T LOSE YOUR IDENTITY 81

RULE #9 BE SAFE, RESEARCH YOUR DATES 90

RULE #10 TRY NEW PLACES & BE MORE APPROACHABLE 101

SUMMARY 114

FINAL THOUGHTS 119

2ND EDITION EXTRA CONTENT 125

ABOUT THE AUTHOR 159

INTRODUCTION

Have you just come back to the dating world and finding it a bit scary out there? Are you the only single one left in your group of friends and can't figure out why? Are you new to the online dating world and don't know where to start? Have your romantic relationships just not turned out the way you envisioned?

If you answered yes to any of these questions, then this is the book for you! I would consider myself an expert at dating by this time in my life. I am currently 34 years old, been engaged twice, and married once. After I divorced who I thought was my soul mate, I really started taking a new look at my romantic relationships and why they just weren't going in the direction I thought they would be. I stopped blaming everyone else for my bad romances and finally started to look inside myself. My dating history had one common, painfully obvious factor: me. Going back into the dating world, I didn't want to do another repeat of my marriage. I had truly thought I found my life partner at the time and was rudely awakened when it didn't turn out the way I dreamed it. I knew I really needed to dig deep down inside myself to find the roots of my romantic problems. I was finally going to put a stop to the broken record of bad romances. I was finally going to have the relationships I always dreamed of. I deserved it, and I was going to make it happen!

As I ventured out into the scary dating world of fakes, freaks, and fanatics, I soon remembered why I wanted to be married in the first place. The dating world is more like a jungle. Before you venture out, you need to be armed with wisdom, courage, strength, and possibly some mace. Strap a few cans of pepper spray to your Gucci belt, clip a few throwing stars on your Prada heels, throw some face paint on, and use your oversized Coach bag as your shield. You are ready to endure the beasts in the jungle!

Okay, well, maybe it's not that bad, but mace isn't a bad thing to carry! You do have to be careful out in the dating jungle because you just don't know who you're going to meet. There's the guy who's only looking for a good time, and after you sleep with him, he'll never call you again. Follow that with the garden-variety liars, cheaters, con artists, druggies, married ones, and straight-up psychopaths. It almost makes a girl just want to stay home every night with a bottle of wine, a couple packs of cookies, and a box set of Sex and the City. Even as wonderful as that sounds, you're definitely never going to find Mr. or Mrs. Right by sitting on your couch at home eating cookies. You have to take life by the stirrups. Get out there and live it!

Once I decided to start going on dates, I started setting rules for myself to follow so I wouldn't slip back into my old dating habits. If a date didn't go well, I would reflect on it afterwards and develop a new rule. I wasn't going to let all these bad dates go to waste. They were field research. Learn from the bad, improve, and move on. I starting writing my rules, and this was how the book was born. As I discussed my dating problems with my other girlfriends, I noticed we were encountering a lot of the same issues. These rules are a group effort—a combination of our experiences out in the jungle. There are quality guys and girls out there. You and I are quality people, right? If you follow these rules they will help you navigate through the scary jungle, bypassing the snakes and lizards to find your loving Tarzan or Jane.

RULE #1

HEAL ALL YOUR WOUNDS FIRST BEFORE LOVING ANOTHER

This is the most important rule in the entire book. It is why I put it before all the others. It is very important that you master this rule before you go on to any other rule in the book. It may take you a couple of weeks or months, and that's okay. Take your time with it. How many wounds need healing will dictate how long you need. This isn't a race, so don't rush it.

As has been said many times over, you can't love someone else if you don't love yourself. How can you expect to give someone else love if you can't give it to yourself first? In order to love yourself, you need to heal any emotional wounds that you have endured over your lifetime. These can be any bad relationships in your life—boyfriends, husbands, fathers, brothers, mothers, close friends, et cetera. The first relationships that you develop with your immediate family during adolescence have a huge impact on your dating life and how you perceive an intimate relationship should function.

This is my first rule in the dating jungle because if you don't start off on a positive place within yourself, none of the other rules will matter. You would only be building the rules on very shaky foundations. If you had just one bad relationship and learned from it, that's great. That's how it should be. You realize that's what you *didn't* want in a partner and went for the opposite in another. This is healthy, growing and developing in the right way. If you've been in a string of bad relationships, one after another, you need to start taking a look inside yourself. I did.

I had three major relationships in my life that were pretty much all the same, just different jerks. They might as well have been the same guy with different faces and addresses. The definition of insanity is doing the same thing over and over again and expecting a different result. After my marriage ended I thought I was going insane. I couldn't believe how I kept finding these crazy guys. What was wrong with me? I thought to myself, *I'm attractive, intelligent and down-to-earth. Why can't I find a normal guy?* I really thought maybe all guys were jerks, or that I just deserved this. Maybe love just wasn't in the cards for me. It seemed like everything else in my life was perfect, besides finding love.

Before we called it quits on our marriage, we tried going to marriage counseling together to see if we could work it out. My husband, we'll call Lou, only made it to 2 sessions, and then we decided to file for divorce. I decided to stay and continue therapy. I figured I was going to need it to help me through the devastation of divorce, and it couldn't hurt, right? I used the time to talk about why Lou was so bad. I complained about how rude he was; inconsiderate, unfaithful, and a liar. I figured she would agree with me since she had already met him and knew what I was going through. Instead she just looked at me calmly and asked why I was letting him treat me this way. She told me I was a smart, level headed person; why would I let someone manipulate me?

I wasn't sure. I never really stopped to think of it like that. I was always putting the blame on him—he did this to me, and I'm the victim. This started to turn my thinking in a new direction. We stopped focusing on Lou and starting focusing on me. I went from being a passive actor in my own life to running the script.

Over the next five months of therapy, I came to the realization that the relationship I had with my father wasn't all puppy dogs and fairytales like I thought it had been. At this point in my life, my father and I were actually really close. It hadn't always been that way. When I was about 3, my mother and father divorced. I didn't know why at the time, and I still don't know all the details. But when I was older my father did confess to me after a few drinks one night that he was unfaithful. After the divorce, he moved about 3 hours away, to a bigger city. He would come around every now and then, though I remember not wanting to go spend time with him. For about the next 10 years I really don't have any memories of him being around. My mother put herself through school and eventually got a teaching job in the city where my father was living. We ended up buying a house within close proximity of him. It was then, around when I was 12, that he starting participating in our lives more often, but the relationship was still rocky.

My mom was very busy working and raising two kids, so home-cooked meals were rare. We usually went out for dinner to fast food restaurants. The extra calories didn't sit well on my already large frame. During adolescence I was very tall. Adding extra pounds to an abnormally tall body did not help my self-esteem. I never fit in with the others kids. I was bigger, taller I stuck out like a sore thumb. I didn't have many friends during adolescence. We moved around a lot and I always wanted to just blend in or be a fly on a wall. Instead I was always rumored about that I was actually a teacher and not an actual student. My father would take my brother and me to the gym to work out. I felt awkward being in a place that was for adults. I would look around at all the beautiful, skinny women jogging in their cute shorts and sports bras. I wore baggy clothing to cover up my ugly body. I was embarrassed to even be there. I would quickly walk a few minutes on the treadmill, then tell me father I was done with my workout and would wait for him in the lobby. I'll never forget the words he spoke to me next. He looked at me with disgust in his eyes and said, "You're already done? How can you be done? You know someday you're going to have to work out." My already low self-esteem plunged even lower. That sentence right there spun me into an entire life long eating disorder, workout addiction and body image distortion.

When I was 16 I started working for my dad part-time after school. He had developed his own real estate company and was becoming somewhat successful. I was doing his bookkeeping for him, posting rents and paying bills for a few different properties he had. When it came time for a paycheck, he would always make me ask him for money instead of keeping track of my hours. Every time the amount would be different, so I never knew how much I was going to get. If he had given me money two weeks prior he would ask what I spent it on and why I needed more. It was hard to budget for things such as gas and clothes. I finally decided working for my father wasn't the best thing, so I got part-time jobs at other places.

During my senior year in high school I got into drinking and drugs pretty heavily. My mom would have a fit over everything I did. We would get into huge fights and I would leave the house. I got pretty bad, skipping classes and not prepping for my ACT exam. I even got arrested a couple of times for possession and theft. My mom was devastated. She tried to discipline me the best she could all by herself. I didn't really pay attention to any of it and just did whatever I wanted to. My dad never really had much to say during those times. I only remember him telling me, while he was driving me to my court appointment for possession, "Just don't buy it yourself or hold onto it. Let your friends carry the dime bag."

For my freshman year of college, my dad paid for me to go to University of Nebraska at Lincoln, home of the Cornhuskers. He wanted me to have the university experience. I didn't really care where I went, because I knew I was being groomed to take over the family business. My life was planned out for me without my opinion as to what I wanted to do with it. I spent most of those college days drinking and getting high, self-medicating into oblivion. I was trying to drown out the pain, which I didn't even know existed at that time. Halfway through my freshman year I had an epiphany, or maybe it was an alcohol and drug induced hallucination. Laying in the middle of my dorm room floor everything to me seemed clear as day: I couldn't keep doing this to myself and my body. I couldn't keep living life in a haze. The next day I quit drugs, cold turkey. I finished out my first year of college, then went onto receive a degree in graphic arts from a community college.

After graduating college and being out in the workforce for a few years, I already had a string of bad relationships: a college boyfriend that didn't really work out, an engagement that never even really got off the ground. I was still trying to date and find the right guy for me. Most of my girlfriends were already married or engaged. Some were even having babies! By Midwestern standards I was becoming an old hag. Most people were married by 25. We had Christmas that year at my dad's house. I was already feeling depressed about my love life when I opened a present from him. I sat in the living room with my mom, brother, aunt, cousin, grandma, and stepmom all watching me. Our tradition was to pass out presents and then each person opens a present one by one. That way, we all get to see what everyone got. I tore open the wrapping paper to reveal a book. I turned it over to reveal a cover that had a cartoon picture of a girl upside down in a trash can. The title was *Stop Getting Dumped*. I felt the tears well up in my eyes. I could barely lift my head to look around at everyone without bawling. When I did I looked at my father, he had his back turned to me, cocktail in hand and laughing hysterically. I still to this day don't understand how he found that funny. When I got back to my house, I cried myself to sleep.

Shortly after that Christmas I moved to Florida. I had always wanted to live by the water, with a warmer climate and beaches. I was miserable in Nebraska. I was depressed all the time. I had a high-paying job, nice house, car, all my family and friends lived there . . . I just felt like a piece of me was missing. I just wasn't happy. Then on December 31, 2002, I was laid off from my job. I had a girlfriend living down in the Tampa Bay area and I really wanted a change of scenery. It seemed like the perfect time to leave. So I packed everything in my car and drove down. I fell in love immediately. The warm sun on your skin, the salty breeze from the ocean, the beautiful palm trees—I had arrived in paradise!

I lived in Florida for about a year when my father told me he was looking to invest in real estate there. He told me to look for a place, he would purchase it, and I would pay the bills to live there. *Fantastic idea*, I thought. I started looking around at properties. This was right around the peak of the market, so property was going like hotcakes.

I found a beautiful condo by a golf course that I fell in love with. We drew up the papers, my father purchased the condo, and I moved in. It was a nice 3-bedroom unit, pretty large and spacious, allowing me to move all my furniture from Nebraska down to Florida. I then started looking for roommates and began to rent out bedrooms in the condo. I had multiple roommates. I listed the rooms for rent, interviewed the tenants, ran background checks, wrote up leases, and handled deposits—pretty much the basic job of a property manager.

My father continued to purchase rental properties within the Florida area as the years went on. He bought a little condo close to the beach and eventually the house that Lou and I lived in while we were married. I continued to manage all the properties that he acquired in the Florida area. I handled everything from major maintenance issues (even though I wasn't licensed or certified), to garbage disposals, to changing door locks once a tenant moved out. I even handled an eviction of 2 girls from beginning to end; everything from speaking with the attorney and serving notice of eviction to dealing with local law enforcement. Over time I was learning and becoming even more involved in my father's business. It was a lot of work because I still had another job to pay my bills. I did the real estate on the side, believing I was doing it just for the pure experience since I wasn't getting paid. After about 7 years I decided to get my Florida Real Estate License. Once I was licensed, I discovered what a real estate agent actually made for their work, and it dawned on me that my father wasn't paying me for the work I was doing for him. I felt ripped off. At that time I was managing 3 rentals and doing all of the work. My father was only paying me one flat fee, which wasn't anything near the standard. Never mind that I had been doing this for the past 7 years, he had only been paying me a small fee for the last year. I was very frustrated because I only had time for a part-time job, since all these other real estate duties were taking up my time. At the time, Lou and I were having financial issues. I couldn't afford to pay for much and he wanted me to get a full-time job. If I got a full-time job, I couldn't help out with the real estate. I was in a bad predicament and it caused major stress within our marriage.

On top of all that, I didn't feel appreciated for my efforts. My father never really said he wanted me in the business or wanted me to help run it. It was just kind of a given. One weekend Lou, my good friend, my father, and I were driving down to Miami. I was driving the car in a really bad rainstorm; we had just picked up my father from the airport. I'm not sure exactly what the conversation was about at the time, though the only thing I do remember is my father saying: "When your brother was diagnosed with leukemia and epilepsy when he was little, I was so sad. I had always wanted my son to take over the family business." I looked at him in the rearview mirror waiting for a follow up, something along the lines of, "But I have an intelligent daughter so that's great." Or, "I'm glad one of my children can take over the business." Nothing but silence filled the air, a deafening silence that sliced right through my heart.

Growing up, it was implied that I would inherit the real estate properties and manage them. Especially since my brother had a debilitating disease that wouldn't allow him to. I never really stopped to think what I wanted to do with my life, or thought that it didn't really matter. Whatever I tried, I could fail everything, and this would always be there to back me up.

After I got divorced, I wanted to do to do real estate full-time. Once we moved out of our house, I had to move in with my father at his house on the beach in Florida because I had all of our other properties rented. We were in the process of starting a real estate company together. I was really happy and thought it was all going to work out great. Now that I was doing real estate full-time I could get paid the standard fees, right? The next two months that followed were anything but great.

I had never lived with my father prior to this time after my divorce at 33 years old. I only had when I was a baby, but I lived with my mother when my parents divorced. He was in and out of my life but we didn't really get along until after I graduated college. Then we were really close as I believe he was trying to make up for time lost when I was younger. Over compensating with extravagant gifts and money Since we had been getting along pretty well the last 10 years, I figured it wouldn't be that big of a deal living with him for a while.

During the day we would work out of his house. He had his office in a room and I had my office in part of the living room. As I was busy working away, my father would walk by and abruptly drop something on my desk, saying, "Here's something for you to do." Irritated, I would drop everything I was doing to help him. Most of the time it wouldn't even have anything to do with business; it would be something like a mistake on his cable bill. I would have to call and sit on hold for 2 hours while he did something else. Then one day his computer broke down and got some bad viruses. I spent 12 hours reformatting his hard drive, reinstalling the operating system, putting back all his software, and getting it to function properly—all without any kind of thank you. Forget any kind of computer repair fees, all he did was complain that none of his bookmarks were there in Internet Explorer. I couldn't even get any work done because every five minutes he would yell from his office and ask me to help him open this file or print this off or install this. I got to the point where I would just leave for hours on end and just go to the pool or Starbucks by myself because I couldn't take it anymore. I was working around the clock on everything from stuff on the house, to his computer, to driving him around everywhere. Meanwhile, I wasn't getting any more fees than I had before. I was basically his personal slave.

He spent most of his time installing a hot tub he purchased. He was putting it together all by himself out in the Florida heat. He would do anything to spare a nickel, even if it meant giving him a heart attack, just so he wouldn't have to pay anyone to help him. This stemmed from growing up poor on a farm. He would work outside in the heat all morning, then come inside to make himself a salad and couple glasses of red wine for lunch. Then it was back to work outside, followed by a few beers to cool off. Usually around 4 came nap time, and after that, the alcohol really started flowing. It would usually begin with a few margaritas, then maybe some Crown Royal on ice. About 9, right after the sun went down, he would go sit in the hot tub. Of course, he had a big drink in hand on the way out.

I now understand why they put warnings on hot tubs to not drink alcohol while you're soaking. After an hour of sitting in there, he would stumble out so drunk he would turn mean. He would come inside and yell at me because he didn't like the television show I was watching or some other stupid thing. I finally got into the habit of going into my room, turning off the light, and watching my TV on low after he went outside so he thought I was sleeping. He would usually pass out somewhere in the house, but sometimes around 2 or 3 AM I could hear the ice falling from the machine into a glass and I knew he was making more drinks.

We started arguing all the time. Anytime I had a difference of opinion or wanted to do something my way and stand up for myself, he would throw his hands in the air and grumble, "I guess I don't know anything!" I felt like I had ended one bad marriage just to move right into another one. I was miserable. During one of my therapy sessions it hit me like a ton of bricks: *I married my father!* Not literally, but figuratively. I was subconsciously trying to win the approval of my father through the men that I was dating. All the men I choose had all the bad characteristics of my father. I was inadvertently telling myself that I didn't deserve the love from a caring, honest, trustworthy man. Instead, I kept finding the cheaters and liars who didn't care about my needs. It was all about them. I kept trying to win their approval over and over and over again. I was on a downward spiral.

Not until I uncovered this important key information was I able to start turning my life around. It was hindering me from being successful in every aspect of my life, even my career. I thought for years I wanted to be in real estate, but then I realized I wasn't sure if I did anymore. That was my father's dream, that was his empire, and I was just a pawn in the scheme to help him be successful. Why was I working for free? Because I was trying to win his approval and make him happy. It sure as hell didn't help *me* any. I couldn't even put it anywhere on my resume because half the time I wasn't even doing legitimate work. So just how was this advancing my career? Was this even what I really wanted to do with my life? I always figured I had to, that it wasn't really a choice, but it was a choice. It was my life.

I finally had to confront my father, stand up to him, and tell him what I needed if I was going to stay in business with him. I couldn't be treated like a slave any longer. I deserved to get paid like every other licensed real estate agent. It was the most courageous and most terrifying thing I have ever done in my life. Standing up to my father and telling him exactly how I felt and what I wanted was something I had never done before. Whatever he wanted, I agreed to it. Whatever beliefs he had, I agreed with him. I never stood up for myself. I once and for all had to look fear straight in the eye and say, *"To hell with you, I'm looking out for me now."*

I never will forget that rainy morning in Nebraska. I had come back for a week visit to see my friends and family. My brother and I drove to a quaint little breakfast café to meet my father. My father had left Florida to go back to Nebraska over the summertime. So I had not seen him in about a month. During that time I had typed up an agreement for the terms and conditions that I wanted met if we were going to stay in business together. It essentially read that I would get paid a fee when I leased a unit, which in Florida is a typical first month's rent. I would also be paid a maintenance fee each month to do property management. I would not fix appliances for which I was not qualified, such as AC units, water heaters, et cetera. I would be paid a cleaning fee after a unit was vacated or hire a cleaning crew. Completely legit contract for services rendered. I had not spoken to my father much prior to this meeting. I knew I was being taken advantage of, and I wasn't happy about it, but it was hard to tell him. I wanted to do it in person.

My brother, father, and I sat down for breakfast. I knew my father could tell I wasn't the same person inside as I was before. I could see it in his eyes. It was awkward and I was so nervous. I didn't know when or how I was going to bring it up. I couldn't even really listen to the conversation that was going on at the table because I was pre-occupied with trying to decide when to confront him. We ordered breakfast but I couldn't eat it. I felt like I was going to throw up. My father started bringing up business topics, pretty much the only thing that we ever really discussed. I decided it was now or never. I reached into my purse and pulled out my contract. With shaky hands and a wary voice, I told him I wanted to discuss some things. I started reading the contract and he put his head down towards his plate. "I'm not even going to acknowledge that," he said. I was shocked that he would say such a thing, but decided to just keep going and proceeded onto to the second clause slowly. Before I could finish he exploded, "I can't believe you're doing this to me, after everything I've done for you! I'm going to spend all my money before I die so you won't see a goddamn cent! I'm taking you out of my will. You could've had everything!"

I started shaking uncontrollably. Tears were falling so quickly, they dropped off my cheeks and landed in my omelet. I couldn't believe the words that he was saying to me, his only daughter. All I wanted was to just be treated like a normal real estate agent. My therapist tried to prepare me for what I was going to encounter, but there wasn't enough mental preparation for that. She kept telling me I couldn't expect rational behavior from an irrational person. For him, it was his way or the highway. Through my tears I said, "I don't want anything from you." I grabbed my purse and got out of the restaurant, leaving my brother and breakfast behind.

I drove back to my mother's house bawling, tears streaming down my face. I really just couldn't grasp all that had just happened. I truly thought it would have gone better. I was really hoping deep down inside somewhere there would be a small chance we would be able to have a normal conversation. That he would listen to me and accept me as a smart, grown business woman and not treat me like a pathetic child.

That was the moment when I realized my father was not the perfect person I had always made him out to be. It opened my eyes to the harsh reality that I glossed over—all his flaws, harsh judgments, and verbal abuse. I had put him on a pedestal of make believe.

My father had to bring my brother back to my mother's house after they finished eating. He called me on my cell phone and asked me to come out to the car. He spoke more calmly this time around, but there still was no getting through to him, since he didn't understand my proposal. He said he couldn't pay the fees, but he could give me an additional monthly flat amount. That wasn't what I was asking for, I just wanted to get paid for each job I did. He then reminded me that he paid for my college tuition, which had nothing to do with the conversation at hand. I wasn't aware that someone paying for my college meant I was a servant to them for the rest of my life. If I would have known that was the case when I was 18, I would of taken out a student loan. I said being in business together wasn't going to work out and that I was handing all my real estate responsibilities back to him. He was in shock. He smirked and asked, "What are you going to do then? You think you're going to make money by drawing, painting and writing?!"

"Yes, that's exactly what I'm going to do," I responded quietly as I left the car.

OVERVIEW: Rule #1

- Heal ALL wounds before you love another. It doesn't matter if they came from a past divorce, an old romance, or even a traumatic childhood.

- You're damaged goods and won't be able to see things clearly going into the dating jungle until you heal yourself.

- Get therapy if you need to and take all the time you need.

RULE #2

DON'T DATE ANYONE WHO IS MARRIED

I know that this tip seems like a no-brainer. *Gee, why would I date a married guy?* Most people don't intentionally go out looking for a married person. Some do, and those people definitely need even more help than this book can offer. If you are intentionally seeking out a married person, you have *deep* issues going on. Therapy might have to come into play on that one.

What I'm talking about here is when, for example, a woman meets a guy online whose internet profile says he is single or divorced, yet he's actually married. Or you meet a guy in a club and he doesn't have on a wedding ring. He fails to tell you he's married until after he's got you hooked with some hot chemistry. Then he says his relationship is on the rocks just to keep you around, but they're still living together for the sake of the kids. He keeps feeding you lines of BS because he wants to have his cake and eat it too. These are the guys you have to watch out for.

The reason why I'm putting this as Rule #2 is that in the last few months I was surprised at how many of my single girlfriends and I were getting duped by married guys. This seems to be an ongoing issue with innocent women who are not intentionally going out there to "find" an unavailable man. Unfortunately, infidelity does go on in this world and you don't want to get caught in the middle of a tangled web.

When I first met Lou, his online profile stated that he was divorced. It started off as a whirlwind romance filled with long dates of candlelight dinners, exotic trips, and shopping sprees. We spent almost every day together for the first few months. If we were not physically in each other's presence, then we were on the phone talking or texting. I felt totally secure and safe within our relationship. About two months into our relationship, I met his brother for the first time. We were out for dinner in a fancy restaurant in the Brickel district of Miami. As we were seated at our table, sipping wine, his brother walked in the front door. Lou took that moment to lean over to me and whisper in my ear, "Oh by the way, I'm still married." My eyes opened wide with rage as I seethed, wanting to punch him in the face. Yet, I had to restrain myself from the wrath of my own fury because I had to make a good impression on his brother. I swallowed down my disgust, put on a smiling face, and shook his brother's hand.

Throughout the night I put on a performance worthy of an Academy Award, pretending that everything was fine. That I had not just discovered my new boyfriend was married to someone else. Of course, Lou thought he was off the hook, since he so cowardly divulged that important information at such a time I couldn't attack him. That just made my rage boil deep down inside for way too long, until we were alone. I played nicely until the end of the night. As soon as his brother left for the evening, I let him have it. *What do you mean you're married? You said you were divorced! Why would you lie to me, what the hell is going on?* He just fired back and said I was so upset because I had too much to drink. He turned it around on me, trying to make me feel guilty for a situation he caused. But the drinks had nothing to do with it and the lying had everything to do with it. We argued until the early morning. I was so upset I walked outside to the ocean at 4 AM. I just sat there by myself letting the cold waves rush over my feet, thinking, *Who the hell is this person?*

The following day, he explained that the divorce was taking so long because of his son. They were trying to get him diagnosed with autism, the state makes it very hard, and even more difficult if the parents are going through a divorce. It seemed like a legit explanation, that he was doing this for his son's sake. Since I have seen firsthand the difficulties and paperwork my mother endured with my brother's own disability, I thought there might be some truth to what he was telling me.

In the following months of our relationship, I met his son, his family, and his "wife." As time went on I became closer to his young son, whom I adored as if he was my own child. Since his "wife" lived 4 hours south of us I really wasn't concerned at the time that he was going to go back to her or anything of that nature. Our relationship was moving forward, we were happy, and everything seemed to be on track.

After about 7 months of dating, Lou proposed to me. I was excited and happy. Our relationship had been going so well at that point. He said I was his soul mate, that he was working on the details of divorce, and it wouldn't take that much longer. He only wanted to be with me, I was the one, his best friend. He had never imagined he could find someone with whom he could be so close with and bare his soul to. My friends got along well with him and my cousin considered him like family already. I was 31 years old and ready to finally settle down in my life. Everything was perfect, besides that one little nagging thing: he was still married to someone else.

Of course I couldn't tell anyone about it, but they would have probably knocked some much-needed sense into my head. I was living in my fairytale. I wanted my happily-ever-after, damn it! All my girlfriends had been married for a long time by now, most of them with kids, and here I was still single! I really thought it was my time to shine. My fairytale would come true. So I strapped on my happy face and continued refining my role in my movie of denial.

After six months of being engaged we moved into the house together. It seemed appropriate since we were going to be married soon. I was happily busy making wedding plans; finding venues, creating invitations, and planning everything down to the nitty-gritty. I didn't hire a wedding planner because I knew I could do it myself better. We had one year to get ready for the most fabulous wedding in history. It was going to be on the beach at the historic five-star Don Cesar. Everything was going to be executed precisely down to the cummerbunds of the ring bearers.

The only one thing standing in the way of our perfect wedding was the tiny, itty-bitty problem of my groom still being legally married to someone else. Since clearing that up was his only task, I figured it wouldn't be a problem. One year to finalize a divorce. In Florida there is no waiting period like in some other states. It's pretty quick as long as neither party is fighting, which they were not, so it should have been a piece of cake.

As I preoccupied myself with fine-tuning all the details of the wedding stuff, I tried to deny what was really going on: *I'm planning a huge wedding to a guy who isn't even legally available to be married.* I would ask him about it every now and again. *How's it coming? Has the attorney called back? Where are the papers? What's going on?* He would just get angry at me for asking these simple questions. Excuses were the only things coming out of his mouth. The attorney won't return his phone calls, they need this, they need that, or he don't have time to deal with this.

About two weeks prior to our big extravagant event, he was still married. I was in panic mode. What was I going to do? *This isn't happing to me. We have 150 people flying in from all over the US. Full fees have already been paid to the vendors. There's no way we can reschedule or push this back.* As if the stress of planning a wedding wasn't enough, this weight that had been on my shoulders for the last two years was about to throw me into a nervous breakdown. I went into survival mode and came up with a plan. The only item that makes a ceremony legal is the marriage certificate filed with the courts. It's not the flowers, or the dresses, or the cake, or any of that hoopla. It lies within the courts. So we planned to just wait on getting our marriage certificate after the ceremony, and no one had to know. My plan was perfect. If we stayed married for the rest of our lives, as I was planning, this small bump in the road was only a minor detail.

As I stood in front of my wedding guests that February night, the cold air breezing through my long silk wedding gown, holding his hands and saying our vows, I really felt like a was just a little girl playing dress-up in a super-expensive party for all of our friends and family to witness. Of course, nobody had any clue that they were not witnessing a legitimate wedding ceremony. No one had any idea the groom was legally married to someone else. I just kept telling myself it would all be okay, once we got this legal messed straightened out.

After we said our vows, I went from being engaged to a married man to pretending to be his wife. As the months came and went after our fake wedding ceremony in February, the divorce was still dragging on. He kept telling me it didn't matter, it was just a piece of paper. I was his soul mate and we were meant to be together and who really cares. I knew in my heart it wasn't right, but what was I supposed to do? Everyone thought we were legally married! I couldn't tell anyone, because they would know I was a fake and a fraud. I didn't want my fairytale to unravel. I couldn't help it. I had to keep pretending that everything was fine, for everyone else's sake but my own.

As the year started to creep towards the end, we had pretended to be married almost 10 months and he still was not divorced. My outrage was finally coming to the surface. How could a simple divorce take 3 years? This was just insanity! If we let this go on until the New

Year when we file our taxes, we wouldn't be able to file as married. My father's accountant had always done my taxes and he would find out. I was done with the bullshit. "Just get it done," I ordered. Miraculously, once I put my foot down, he finally did.

When he got his final dissolution of marriage papers, I was ecstatic. I was so happy that we could finally be legally married. He, on the other hand, had become very distant and emotionally unavailable. He started working lots of late hours and taking trips to see his son 4 hours away more often without me. I ignored those facts and just wanted legalize our union so I wouldn't be a liar anymore. I wanted to go to the courthouse on a Friday afternoon so we could go out and celebrate after. I mean geeze, we were finally tying the knot! On the other hand, he wanted to do it on a Tuesday or Wednesday. He didn't see the big deal in it. He kept saying our other wedding was the real ceremony and the paperwork didn't mean anything. Well, it meant the world to me, though it was like pulling teeth to get him to comply. I should have realized it didn't matter the day of the week; he just didn't want to be married to me period.

I eventually got him to agree to one Friday afternoon, so I got all dressed up and we went to the courthouse. We finally got our long awaited marriage certificate! I immediately wanted to go to the Melting Pot to celebrate. We were legal! Instead, he wanted to go to Miami for the weekend—by himself. My heart was crushed. He should have been just as excited as me, finally marrying our "soul mates". But in reality, he had just finally caved in to my demands.

Not even a month into our real marriage, we were having problems. We were fighting all the time, everything from the cleaning and cooking to taking care of our cat. We were still newlyweds, yet we were bickering like an old married couple. I was miserable. Why did I fight to legalize this union of insanity? I was so content on making everything legal, I didn't even realize we weren't getting along.

At the end of March, he took a trip to Miami and flat-out said I wasn't invited. It was supposedly a guys' trip to go fishing. His friends were taking him on a long-awaited bachelor party. The funny thing was that in 4 years, I never met any of these so-called friends down in Miami. He would only visit them when I wasn't there. As the trip grew closer, he kept acting weirder and weirder. He got his hair cut like 3 times because they kept doing the fade wrong. He packed so many outfits of nice jeans and shirts it looked like he was going to be gone for a month. Normally, when we went on a trip, he threw a bunch of t-shirts and shorts in a bag just before leaving.

The Sunday he was supposed to be coming back, I called him at 9 AM. His phone rang and went to voicemail. I called back, and it rang twice then went to voicemail. I called again, and then it went straight to voicemail. I called him for 5 hours straight and he never picked up the phone. My heart dropped into my stomach. I felt like I was going to throw up. I just knew something was going on. Something wasn't right. I started to panic and I called all of his family members that lived down there. No one had seen him or knew where he was. Then they all started calling him, so he finally called me, upset that I had called his family. I asked where he had been all this time. He said he was in Starbucks, with no cell reception… for 5 hours.

When he came back from his trip late on Sunday night, he wouldn't look me in the eyes. I was sitting on the couch watching TV when he came in and sat over on the chair. Very cold and distant, like I didn't even know who he was. The next day I made us fajitas for dinner. It was one of our favorite meals to eat. While he was filling his tortillas, I asked him, "Did you cheat on me?"

Surprised, he looked me dead in the eyes and said, "I would never cheat on you. I love you so much, I would never hurt you that way. If I wanted to be with someone else I would just break up with you." The butterflies in my stomach flew away and I actually kind of felt guilty for thinking such things. He was always saying that he was paying the price for what my previous fiancé had done to me. He said I was always overreacting and didn't know how to trust anyone. I started to believe that I couldn't trust my own judgment anymore.

For about 24 hours, our marriage was back on track. Everything was right in the world. Then he called me on Wednesday morning. He said, "I have to tell you something tonight after work." I knew that tone in his voice, and I knew what he was going to tell me. I demanded that he tell me right then. He reluctantly told me that he had an affair.

I starting crying so hard I couldn't breathe. I was hyperventilating. My heart felt like it had just been ripped out of my chest. My mind was racing. I knew in my gut it was true, but my heart wasn't ready to handle it. I felt like I was in a surreal world. My entire life was crashing all around me. The perfect fairytale was turning into a horror movie so fast I couldn't comprehend it.

He immediately came from work to the house. He just sat there on the bed looking at me blankly while I bawled. He just sat there—cold, speechless, with dry eyes. As I drilled him with questions through my panic attacks, he finally admitted he'd met her online. He said it was a one-time thing and he was never going to talk to her again. I didn't believe him. How could I after he lied to me for so long? I couldn't look at him. I was filled with disgust. I had to get out of our house. I couldn't be there anymore, I couldn't stand it. As I started packing my bags, he insisted he didn't want me to go. He said he was the one who should leave, and he wanted to move out. I refused. I packed a huge bag and drove down to my father's house an hour away at the beach.

In the months that followed the truth finally coming out, it was an emotional rollercoaster. First, he would want to work it out, then not. Saying he loved me, and then he wasn't sure, and he wanted to go marriage counseling, then not. We did start therapy, but he only went to two sessions, said he was cured and didn't need to go back. We finally decided to file for divorce. I couldn't handle my life in chaos anymore. I just wanted to be at peace and get off this train that was headed nowhere. Once we filed for divorce, he started his campaign to win me back. He kept telling me how much he loved me and that this other woman didn't mean anything to him. He promised it was a one-night stand. He even went as far as stating that he lied about the affair, that he made it up because he felt uncomfortable living in our house together because my father had purchased it and he didn't. It bruised his ego.

Through all the manipulation to win me back, I stuck to my guns to get divorced. I told him he didn't value the sanctity of marriage and didn't deserve to be married. In the courtroom on the day of our divorce (ours only took 90 days from filling date to final judgment) he sat next to me holding my hand. He was stroking my hair and telling me how beautiful I was. "Let's get out of here," he said. "Let's run far away and pretend that none of this ever happened." A part of me wanted to pretend that nothing had happened and that we would be okay. I never thought I would be divorced, let alone only a few short months after being married.

But I knew I couldn't trust him anymore. I held my ground and we got our final dissolution of marriage from the judge.

After the divorce, Lou texted and called me excessively. I just wanted to move on with my life. But if I didn't answer my phone when he called, he would call every couple of minutes until I did. He emailed photos of me, himself, and his son together. Jokingly, he would ask me when our first date was going to be. He was trying everything to tug at my heart. Not even a week after our divorce, I received an email from a woman claiming to be his fiancée.

A big lump formed in my throat. *His what?*

Just a few hours previously, he and I had just gotten into a fight over the phone. He wanted to take me to dinner and I refused. I frantically read the woman's email on my iPhone, trying to comprehend the small words on the screen and digest what I was seeing. I went to my computer to read it better. The email said she was his fiancée and they had been engaged for a few months. They had been dating for about 5 months and she found out that he was married through a Google search. Of course, he was lying to her, saying that he and I had already filed for divorce, when in reality at that time (5 months ago) we were totally fine.

I was floored. As I read over her email, it was like déjà vu. It was as if I was seeing myself 4 years earlier, when he and I first started dating, the naïve girl believing the lies of a married man. The story repeats itself all over again. I was just happy to not be a part of the picture anymore. Thank goodness I pushed the divorce through as quickly as possible and didn't drag it out for 3 years like he did with his first wife.

If I had followed Rule #2 in the very beginning of our relationship, I could have avoided this entire mess. If a person you are dating is separated, do not get into a serious relationship until you see the final judgment from the courts. Also, if you think the guy you are with might be married and not telling you the truth, do a search via public records. You can find all the information online.

I know some situations may not be as horrific as the one I dealt with, yet I still think this rule applies. Once I filed for divorce and was separated from Lou, it still wasn't a good time for me to be dating anyone. Divorce is one of the hardest things a person can go through in their life. Even if there's no cheating, lying, or manipulation, it's still emotionally devastating. You're not in a good place to try to start up a budding romance with someone new. You need to take the time to heal yourself and be there for your children, if you have any. Take the time to get to know *you* again and be with supportive friends and family.

If you do try to start dating too soon, most likely you are still going to be a broken person inside. It takes time to heal yourself from such a hard event, such as divorce, in your life. No one can just walk away from a marriage without any emotional damage. No one. You don't want to enter another relationship being a vulnerable person. Guys can smell that a million miles away. You'll attract someone who wants you to be weak and frail. Eventually, when you start becoming more like your normal, strong independent self, they will not be happy. They will want to keep you in a sad, pathetic, vulnerable role. That's not healthy for your recovery. Don't get stuck in a cycle of co-dependent relationships.

Take time out to be by yourself. Once you are truly happy to be alone, that's when you can find the right mate. If you're always looking for the next relationship, then you're not happy being alone. It's really not that scary. Some people are afraid they'll end up an old maid, to die alone with their cats. Well, if you don't take the time to truly be 100% happy without a partner in your life, you will die alone anyway.

When you really find out who you are and what you want from life, and are able to put your needs ahead of anyone else's, then you will be able to make a lover happy and have an equal, healthy relationship of give-and-take. I suggest after a divorce, or bad breakup from a long-term relationship, take at least 6 months to a year to be alone. Go pamper yourself and do anything that you have been denying yourself. Get massages, go out to nice dinners with your friends, get manicures and pedicures, or take a cruise. Have fun and enjoy being the wonderful person you are! Once you're truly happy on the inside and out, you will start attracting healthy people.

In the end, I am actually grateful that this happened with Lou. It wasn't until everything blew up in my face for me to hit rock bottom—to finally fall out of my fantasy land and have the hard cold ground of reality smack me in the face. It wasn't easy. It was the worst 6 months of my life, and I literally wanted to die every minute of it. My heart was broken and my soul was shattered. Though that's what it took for me to turn my life around to finally decide once and for all I deserved to be loved. I wasn't going to allow anyone else to treat me like dirt. The whole last 4 years wasn't his entire fault. It takes 2 people to create a dysfunctional relationship. He lied, I believed it. All the red flags were there waving in the wind, I turned my cheek to them—pretended they weren't there when deep down inside I knew all along I was setting myself up for failure. That's the funny thing . . . we as humans will always fulfill our own prophecies, whether we consciously know it or not. If you subconsciously don't think you deserve to be loved you will fulfill that belief. So it's up to you to change and reprogram your subconscious mind. You can do it through therapy, hypnosis, or self-affirmations. It's just like breaking a bad habit. It's just like quitting smoking. It takes a lot if conscious energy and effort, but it's not impossible.

OVERVIEW: Rule #2

- Don't date anyone who is legally married to someone else, even if they are separated and living physically in different places.

- Don't be the "other" woman or man. You deserve someone's complete and undivided attention.

- Be happy with the relationship you have with yourself before moving into another relationship with someone else.

RULE #3

3 STRIKES YOU'RE OUT

You should apply this rule by keeping score on a piece of paper, just like a baseball score. It's pretty similar to tracking a baseball player at bat: they get 3 strikes before their turn is over. The same rules should apply to dating. Keep score of your dates and their behaviors.

Let's say your boyfriend says he has to work late and cancels his dinner plans with you. Later on, your girlfriend texts you and says she sees your guy out at the bar with friends. Obviously, you would be upset because he *said* he had to work late, so did he lie to you to get out of going out to dinner, blowing you off to just see his friends instead? You should talk to him and find out what happened. Maybe he did work late, then co-workers talked him into having drinks later. It's a totally legit excuse, but you're not 100% sure. So keep track of it as strike number 1. Then a few weeks later he says he's at his parents' house visiting relatives when he's really at the beach with some other girls. Strike number 2. He's starting to show a pattern of lying to you. He *could* have another excuse for why that happened, but liars are really good at coming up with lies to cover up lies. Then, finally, he says he has to travel for work for a week when he's actually going on a cruise with people you've never met before. Now you know he's a compulsive liar. Strike 3! He's out of the dating game with you.

No one's perfect—I totally understand that. But if someone shows a pattern of a certain behavior, that's pretty much who they are. Everyone will commit a white lie here or there, like saying your butt doesn't look big at all in those jeans! That's perfectly innocent, but when someone is constantly telling big fibs, then they have a problem. The first time could be a misunderstanding, second time maybe a fluke, but third time means it is in their nature to lie all the time, or they just don't care enough about you to tell you the truth. After the third time, you might as well stop keeping track, because you're just in denial about what's really going on if you let it continue. Nip it in the bud early on.

The best thing to do is write these strikes on a piece of paper, and be as detailed as possible. Write the date, the event, what he said to you, and what really happened. It's better to write it down, because once they start piling up, it will be harder for you to deny the facts when they are in black and white staring up at you from the paper. If you try to just remember in your head, you could forget details, smooth over things, or try to rationalize it in your brain. Hard evidence is also helpful when you need to confront that person. They may try to manipulate details, get you to question your own memory or second-guess your own judgments. A lot of compulsive liars are really good at talking both you and themselves out of anything. For example, you know what the color purple looks like, but he will come along and try to tell you it's actually blue. You'll argue long enough that even though you know its purple, eventually you start to second guess yourself and think, *Hmmmm, maybe I was wrong; maybe this is the color blue.*

This rule can be applied to any aspect of life: if you're contemplating quitting a job, if you're not so sure about a friend's motivations, et cetera. Example: your girlfriend asks you to lunch one day. You drive to the restaurant on time and she's nowhere to be found. She doesn't even answer her cell phone. You think it's odd and hope nothing bad has happened. You eat your lunch alone, wondering what happened. Strike number 1. A few weeks later, the same girlfriend asks if you want to go out for drinks to A new martini bar on Saturday night. You agree and when Saturday night comes around, you spend an hour trying on little black dresses until you find the right one. You do your hair and makeup—you're all dolled up for a night on the town. You call your girlfriend to see what time you're going to meet up and she doesn't answer her phone. You wait in your apartment for an hour, wondering where the hell she is. Of course, you didn't make backup plans, so now everyone else is already out for the night and you're stuck at home. Strike number 2. By this time you may have already decided she is pissing you off and wasting your time. You may not even need another strike, but you're a forgiving person. She says she's sorry for her previous incidents, her phone died, and she didn't have a battery charger. She gives you all kind of excuses. You decide to try to meet her up for a movie that Sunday. You go to the theatre, buy your movie ticket, get some popcorn, sit in the lobby and watch people walk by. None of them is your so-called friend. The previews are starting; you go in and enjoy the movie by yourself. Strike number 3. She's out, she's not your friend. People who care about other people do not waste their time. It's rude and inconsiderate.

You need to establish healthy boundaries of how you're going to let people treat you. Most people will never change in their behavior patterns. You need to decide if that boyfriend, girlfriend, co-worker, or relative has unhealthy behaviors, and whether you're going to let them treat you in ways you don't deserve. People cannot control other people's behaviors. No matter how hard you wish you could, it's impossible, unless you have some super psychic mental powers or superhuman powers from touching a meteorite that fell from the sky. It will just frustrate you over time if you keep getting upset at what other people are doing. The only person you can control is yourself. You can decide that you don't deserve to be lied to, stood up, or taken advantage of. The power is only within you. Look out for number one because no one else is going to have your best interest in hand besides you.

Some behaviors that don't require 3 strikes to throw them out of the ballgame include any physical or verbal abuse. Any signs of this, and game over. No need for him to strike 3 times. Get out ASAP! Don't wait around for a push to turn into a shove, and then broken ribs. Verbal abuse is harder to detect compared to physical. With physical beatings you see scars and bruises. Verbal abuse cuts inside, tearing through your heart and soul. You may not recognize it at first. Someone says something harsh and you wince like you just got pinched. You think maybe it's not a big deal, but then they just keep coming at you. You're not even sure what you did to deserve an attack. Maybe they don't even realize they're doing it? They were possibly brought up in a similar environment where harsh criticism was the norm. If you feel attacked or hurt or just plain bad after having a conversation with them, call them out on it.

Tell them when they call you a blonde, dingbat, or make oink noise at you when you tell them you're trying to lose weight, it hurts your feelings. They may come back and tell you it was a joke, it wasn't meant to hurt. Tell them, joking or not, it's insulting and you won't allow it. If they say you're too sensitive and try to turn it back on you, just walk away. Avoid communicating with that person at all costs. It's not worth the internal bleeding you're going to encounter day in and out if they do not respect your feelings. When your feelings are hurt, it's for a reason, your heart is telling you this isn't right, I don't like the way he's treating me. It's an internal signal. Don't dismiss it or think you are interpreting it wrong. Don't let that person screw up the thoughts in your head. You have a right to feel the way you do. Don't let anyone cut you into pieces. They definitely won't be there to put you back together.

Make a "Good and Bad" List

Another part of this rule, one that I use frequently, is making a list of the good and bad. I'm sure many of you have already practiced this sort of exercise, but for those who haven't, I'll go over it.

Say you've dated someone for maybe just a few dates and are not sure about them quite yet. Or perhaps you've been dating someone for 6 months, or maybe you've even been married for a couple of years, and things are starting to get rocky. The Rule of 3 Strikes may be harder to apply because so much has already happened. You weren't keeping track before and now you're just lost with so many incidents spinning around in your head. The devil's on one shoulder saying bad things that have happened and the angel is on the other reminiscing about all the good times the two of you have had. It's enough to give you a migraine. You're completely torn and don't know how to make a decision. *Do I stay and work it out or do I leave?* When you get stuck in the situation, sit down some place quiet. Get a blank piece of paper and pen. Fold the paper in half the long way, and then write on the left side "Good" and on the right side "Bad." On the "Good" side, write down all the qualities of the person for whom you are having doubts, such as attentive, affectionate, intelligent, listens, likes to travel. Any quality that you think is a good quality that you want in a partner. Then on the "Bad" side, write down qualities that you don't like so much about them. Examples: He has wandering eyes, lies, disrespects you, still hangs out with his ex, et cetera . . . any quality that you don't like.

Try to stay away from superficial qualities like looks, material possessions, or finances. I know those can be good or bad qualities, but try to stay focused on actual behaviors, characteristics and qualities in the person. If you can't come up with qualities yourself, here's a list you can choose from:

10 RULES TO SURVIVE THE DATING JUNGLE

Good

- Attentive
- Affectionate
- Smart
- Listens
- Respectful
- Loving
- Caring
- Polite
- Sensitive
- Patient
- Honest
- Faithful
- Confident
- Has self-control
- Positive outlook on life

Bad

- Jealous
- Low self-esteem
- Negative outlook
- Manipulative
- Liar
- Unreliable
- Doesn't trust you
- Controlling
- Doesn't respect your boundaries
- Rude to you or other people
- Doesn't listen to you or your needs
- Self-centered
- Irrational
- Hot-tempered
- Isn't open with their feelings
- Physically or emotionally abusive

Now that you have a good list of qualities to start with, write them down on your paper. You can add anything else that you think is important to you. Maybe if you share the same religion, if that's a big factor for you, either positive or negative, write it down. List everything down that you can think of. Now take a look at your list. Which side has more qualities? Is the "Bad" category overflowing with items and there are only a few on the "Good" side? Or is the "Good" side outweighing the "Bad?" It really helps to clear your mind to have it all out in black and white, written on a piece of paper. This exercise always helps me when I'm trying to make a decision.

I had gone on 3 dates with a potential suitor. Everything had gone wonderful the first 2 dates. I was really starting to like this guy. On our third date, I had him over for dinner, everything was going lovely, then he made a comment about something that really threw me off guard. I wasn't really sure exactly how to handle it. I had really liked the guy, but then I was contemplating if he really was a decent guy or not. I didn't want to completely dismiss him for one small comment because that would be irrational. Later on the next day, I sat down to make my list. To my surprise, his good qualities outranked the bad by about 18 different qualities. It was obvious that I should give this guy another chance.

There are some bad qualities that completely outweigh any and all good qualities. If your list is full of good qualities and the only bad is that he abuses you physically, it rules out every single good quality on your list. It doesn't matter how attentive or nice he is, in between the physical abuse. Any abuse, physical or mental, is ground for immediate termination of the relationship.

Just like 3 Strikes Rule, utilizing the Good/Bad list can be helpful in all aspects of life. Whenever you're having a hard time about making a tough decision, write the list. See it in black and white on a piece of paper. The answer should just jump right off the page.

OVERVIEW: Rule #3

- 3 Strikes, You're Out! Keep a list of repeat bad behaviors. After 3, kick them off the team.

- Make a list of "Good/ Bad" qualities to help make tough decisions.

- If there are any signs of physical or verbal abuse, once is enough—get out ASAP!

RULE #4

AVOID THE KNIGHT IN SHINING ARMOR

Most little girls grow up watching cartoons of knights in shining armor coming to rescue the damsel in distress. The knight whisks her away from the dark tower to live in his castle with riches, happily ever after. That's a wonderful scenario when you're five, walking around Disney World in your little princess dress and crown on. Once you're 35, you need to put that dream to rest, unless you live in London where princes really do exist. Still, your chances of getting hit by lighting would still be greater.

Don't just wait around like the damsel in distress and wait for someone to come and save you. It seems all romantic and wonderful that some hunky guy will whisk you away and solve all your problems. That is not reality. It's just like wishing you could just pop a pill and lose 40 pounds in a week. You will lose 40 pounds when you eat healthy and exercise, with lots of discipline and hard work over a period of months. If it seems too good to be true, it probably is.

After living in Florida for about a year, I was working at a dead-end job with a mean boss that I hated. It didn't pay that well and I was stressed out, but didn't know what to do. I had to continue going to the office and taking the torture because I had to pay my bills. I was stuck in one of those ruts that a lot people get trapped in. Sometimes reality isn't fun, but you have to do what you have to do.

I was single at the time and didn't have a whole lot of time for dating since I was working to death at my horrible job. I could barely drag myself out of bed in the mornings because I was dreading the day ahead of me. I somehow made it through the 8 hours of my boss yelling and screaming at me all day, to just sit in rush hour traffic at the end of the day, drag myself up 22 stairs, make a TV dinner, sip a couple glasses of wine, and fall asleep early. The next day, I got up and did it all over again.

I eventually starting dating again and met a man I really liked. We started spending every day together. I told him how much I hated my job and he said I should quit. That he would take care of me. He wanted to move into my condo within the first month so he could pay the bills and I wouldn't have to work. He wanted to get married and have children. He wanted a wife he could take care of. He was a strong, sexy man in his paramedic uniform, going out and saving lives every day. I knew moving in with someone so soon wasn't the best idea, though I thought maybe he could save me, too. It's hard to resist a man in uniform. I really wanted out of my current situation and this seemed like the perfect solution.

After moving in together, his car needed a new stick shift. He said he didn't have the money or a credit card to put it on because the limit wouldn't allow it. If I put it on my card, he would pay the monthly bill. He was desperate because he depended on his car to get back and forth to work. Since we were already living together and there was talk of marriage, I figured it wasn't a big deal. Plus, he was paying most of the bills since I wasn't working any longer. He assured me he would pay it back. No problem.

I had never lived with anyone prior to this. I was excited to play house with a man. It all happened very quickly, but I was excited. I was the good little wifey, ironing and starching his shirts, packing his lunch while he would go out in the world and rescue the civilians.

After his long days, he would tell me his heroic stories of what happened that day over a home-cooked meal.

Pretty soon he proposed to me and we were going to be married. I was ecstatic! (This was my second fiancé, prior to my marriage to Lou.) I started planning the wedding and figuring out the details. He was paying the bills and asked for all my pertinent bank account info. I gave it over easily, since we were engaged and going to get married. That's what you do, combine bank account info, right?

Soon, he began working a lot, taking on extra shifts. He was working nights and weekends. Often, he wasn't making it home for dinner anymore. Then he started not coming home at all and said he was working doubles because he needed to help pay for all of our bills since I wasn't bringing in any income. Eventually I was spending every night alone, with a bottle of wine and movies on TBS, wondering where he was.

One day he finally came home in a flight suit and said he got a promotion to be a flight paramedic. It was a big promotion for him and he would be making a lot of money now. However, it meant that he would have to be gone for weeks at a time. I figured it was good for his career. Now I was totally alone and unable to even reach him via cell phone. If I called him, he wouldn't answer. His excuse would be that he was flying or in another country picking up patients and he didn't have coverage. (This was way prior to smart phones.) The scenario went from my knight in shining armor saving me, to us being roommates who never saw each other. I became even more miserable and lonely than I was in my dead-end job. Now I was an at home wife-to-be with no one to take care of. I was totally isolated.

I was checking the mail one day and I got a collection letter from my credit card company. I hadn't been checking my accounts online because he was supposed to be paying the bills. I immediately went to the computer to check that account, and found he had only made 1 payment in the last six months. I started looking in other accounts and there were multiple withdrawals and unauthorized charges for stuff I didn't know about. I started doing more research, and looking up our cell phone bill. When he said he was actually gone off flying, he had been making multiple calls to local phone numbers. When he came back from one of his so called "flights" I checked his phone while he was asleep. I matched the numbers on the bill with his contacts and they were all different women that he was calling daily. Then I rifled through his paramedic jacket and found condoms.

We didn't use condoms because he wanted to have a baby.

I was furious! I couldn't believe he was playing me for a fool. I kicked him out of my condo. He really had nothing to say for himself, since he had been caught red-handed. In the following months everything completely unraveled. The sheriff's department came to my house looking to serve him with contempt of court. Apparently he had a teenage daughter he was paying child support for. That was news to me. I had no idea he had a daughter or was even married before. He had told me all his relatives where dead, and that he had no one. It wasn't that he didn't have any friends or family, it was that no one would talk to him because he was a con-artist. I eventually found out that he had been married 6 times before. He was in prison prior to meeting me for almost beating a man to death in a bar fight. The entire flight paramedic was a lie, apparently that didn't even exist in our area. He made it all up just so he could leave the house for weeks at a time. I didn't even know where he was or what he was doing. He probably got the flight suit on eBay.

My knight in shining armor wasn't looking to save me, he was looking to drain my bank accounts and get whatever he could from me. Thank goodness this entire charade only lasted for about 9 months and I found out before I became his seventh wife. I got out pretty clean besides a few racked up credit cards and a bruised ego.

The lesson I learned from this is that no one can just swoop in and save you. If you're unhappy with things in your life, you need to save yourself. Don't get caught up in the fantasy. Soon enough reality will come rushing back in and knock you on your butt. Keep yourself grounded. When someone comes into your life and says they can make everything better, watch out. Little red bells should go off in your head. Not just one person is going to wave a magic wand and make life better. Yes, falling in love is great, but when it's with the right person. Just remember to keep your feet on the ground when your head starts going off into la la land. Make sure you are making the right conscious decisions even though you're in love.

Every now and then give yourself a reality check. Remove yourself emotionally from the situation and look at it from a third person perspective. Think, in this situation, what would your girlfriend think about this? Or what would someone else, even a stranger think, about this if you told them the story? It's so easy to get caught up in the whirlwind of romance. Guys and girls will say anything to charm someone they like, especially the smooth talkers. I know, I'm a sucker to fall in love, too. I fall fast and I fall hard. Sometimes without really taking the time to see if this person is as wonderful as they tell me they are. Actions speak louder than words. Watch out for the little things they do, not the big stories they tell. That is what really sets people apart. Anyone can talk a good line of BS, but what do they actually *do* about it?

OVERVIEW: Rule #4

- Avoid the person who wants to save or rescue you; save yourself.

- Actions speak louder than words.

- Get your head out of the clouds and give yourself a reality check every now and then.

RULE #5

LOST PUPPY SYNDROME

Do you always feel like you're rescuing someone? Do your boyfriends or girlfriends always end up being the people who don't have a job or a place to stay? Are your relationships more like helping the needy versus being with someone who's your equal? Then you probably suffer from the lost puppy syndrome. You have an overwhelming need to rescue people, to help them out in some way. My mother used to tell me that when I was younger I was always helping people out, trying to rescue them. I was always hanging out with people who were less fortunate. I would want to give them my clothes and other things from our house. I'm just a naturally giving person. Let me first clarify that there's nothing wrong with helping others, just as long as you're doing it in healthy ways, such as volunteer work, pitching in at the local soup kitchen, or giving clothes to homeless. That kind of helping is fine. It's when your helping flows over into your romantic relationships where it can become unbalanced. You wouldn't marry the homeless guy downtown just to give him food and shelter, right?

Don't take in needy boyfriends or girlfriends the way you might take in a stray dog. This is the opposite of the Knight in Shining Armor fantasy. Instead of wanting to be rescued, you are the one trying to do the rescuing. What happens when you consistently try to rescue people, help them out, then form a relationship from it is that eventually you will soon tire of this person. You're the one with the good job, income, and house. You take in the poor waitress who's struggling to get a start in life. You have a college education; she didn't graduated high school. You can carry on intelligent conversations; she's more about partying and going out. Maybe she never really gets herself off her feet and then you start to feel resentful and think she is just taking advantage of you. Eventually the relationship ends because you're not on the same page.

In a relationship, it's easier to be with someone who's your equal, so you have things in common. Either you've both gone to college or are successful in your careers. Maybe you're bilingual and wish to have someone who also can speak multiple languages. Or you're just a simple person that enjoy simples things and you don't travel much out of your comfort zone. Being with someone who travels all over the world may not be the best person for you. Seek out someone who is somewhere on the same playing field as yourself, and it will make a relationship that much richer.

When you date down—that is, date someone who's not on the same level as you—it's a defense mechanism. You're protecting yourself from actually finding true love and possibly getting hurt in the process. In dating down, you *know* the relationship will go nowhere. Eventually you will tire of this person. Sometimes they even know they're not up to your level and will wonder why you're giving them the time of day. They eventually learn they will never be able to live up to your standards or give you the things you want and need in a relationship. They may even break up with you first because they know they will never get to your level and see it as a roadblock, so they just cut to the chase.

There has to be some level of equality. It's not always tit for tat, but some kind of balance is necessary. Maybe one person is better looking than the other, yet you are both very intelligent and can stimulate each other that way. Whatever makes you feel as if you're with your equal. If you're always feeling sorry for the person, that's not a good start.

It's okay to help someone out in need, there's nothing wrong with that. Just don't use it as the foundation for a relationship. It creates an imbalance between the two people and can create power struggles. One doesn't like that the other is always paying for stuff. It may make the other feel emasculated, or less of a person. Finances are one of the largest issues in relationships. If you're with someone who makes significantly more money than you or vice versa, you should openly discuss it to make sure both parties are okay with it. Some men don't like women being the breadwinners and others are ok with it. Of course, having equal jobs and income would be perfect, but that doesn't always happen. If you want to be a stay at home mom, make sure you discuss it with your partner. Maybe you want to stay home, but he doesn't think he can pay all the bills with his salary. Or possibly he wants you to stay home and you want to have a career. These are huge life issues that you need to be able to openly discuss.

Being on a somewhat equal intelligence level is, for me, very important. You don't have to have scored the same on your ACT test, but just being on the same brain wave is crucial. Everyone is on different levels, mentally. Finding someone who's on yours, to me, is more important than looks. Beauty fades, bodies wrinkle, but minds stay around longer (unless one gets Alzheimer's). It's hard to communicate with people who are not on your same level. You know the co-worker who just never understands your memos, the friend that never gets your jokes, or your roommate you know you can only discuss simple surface topics with. Find someone who gets you and is on your same mental awareness. If you date someone who is on a significantly lower intelligence level than yourself, it can cause the other party to try to dumb you down. They may feel threatened by you and then make you feel incompetent by throwing out small hurtful remarks. They just feel insecure, but that's no way to treat someone. An intelligent person wouldn't have to dumb you down. They would be happy for you and possibly admire you. Equal intelligence will come in handy when you have important things to discuss such as refinancing your house, where to invest money, or what schools are best for your kids.

Finding a person within a certain age range is also equally important. A good rule of thumb is no more than 10 years either older or younger than you. You want to try to at least be in the same generation—or somewhere close to it. Otherwise, you will have nothing in common. When there's a 20 year age gap, you're going to find it difficult to agree on certain topics or even know what the other may be talking about. Different generations have different morals and values. From my experience lots of men have this fantasy of dating women in her early 20s no matter how old they are themselves—40, 50, 60. It just doesn't make sense. You'll want to discuss the economy and she'll want to listen to her iPod. There are certain things that develop as you mature and age. Someone who hasn't even graduated college is not an ideal match for someone who has been working in the real world for 20 years, paying a mortgage and bills. You'll eventually feel like you're taking care of a child. Yeah, she might be young and hot, but looks fade. The only thing that lasts is conversation, laughter, and emotional connections.

It goes in the reverse too, lots of cougars are out there looking for young hot guys. These relationships usually don't last long either. Look at Ashton Kutcher and Demi Moore. They lasted only 6 years in their marriage with their 15-year age difference. Yeah, Demi was hot when they first got together, but after a while her looks faded, too. Consider the age difference: when she's 60, he'll be 45. He'll still be in his prime and she'll be going through menopause. In non-celebrity terms, within an age gap of that sort, your significant other will be almost ready for retirement and you'll be in the grind of your career. They'll want to relax and travel and you'll still be working away. Finding someone who's within an acceptable ago range will allow you to grow old together. When you're both in your 80s, sitting in your rocking chairs old and wrinkled together, you can hold each other's hands and make each other laugh. That's the greatest gift of all.

OVERVIEW: Rule #5

- Don't date down; find someone who's your equal.

- Date within an acceptable age range—no more than 10 years younger or older.

- Find someone who gets you and is on the same intelligence level.

RULE #6

RESPECT YOURSELF & YOUR BOUNDARIES

Respect yourself and all others will follow. You set the rules for how people are going to treat you. Don't waver from your rules! You are the most important person in your life. If you don't take care of yourself, no one else will. Many times relationships can be like little kid—they will constantly push your boundaries to see where you draw the line. If you don't draw the line, they will keep pushing. You know when your boundaries are being tested when you start feeling uncomfortable.

This rule also applies to friendships, family ties, and professional relationships, not just dating. Don't let anyone take advantage of you or push your boundaries. Many of people are only looking out for their best interests and not your own. Say a friend wants you to take a trip somewhere with them, but that person insists on you driving and doesn't even offer to help pay for gas. You give in because they complain their car isn't in good shape. Then they want you to pay more than your share of the hotel room because they are short on cash. Then they get a couple of discounted tickets to go to a park and don't even offer one to you. Instead, you get to pay full price. Your friend isn't really much of a friend if they keep taking advantage of you like this. You need to be the one to put a stop to it. Remember: it takes two people to make a dysfunctional relationship.

With some people, you have to put your foot down and say enough is enough. You are the one in control of how people treat you. If you keep letting someone do this to you, you'll be unhappy and ticked off, but it's your own fault. Draw the line, stand up for yourself and say no. It sounds easy, but it's harder than you think. Especially if you're like me; I would give someone the shirt off my back. Unfortunately, there are people that will keep taking your generosity to the point where they think they deserve it when they have done nothing to obtain it. I call this entitlement syndrome. They believe they are entitled to everything that everyone else has, but won't lift a finger to do it for themselves.

Another important boundary is intimacy. When you first start dating someone, it's key to keep yourself from having sex until you know what kind of relationship you and your partner are looking for. It's especially important to not have sex on the first few dates. Most guys will try to push your boundaries and see if they can get you to sleep with them right away. It's partially flattering knowing that they're attracted to you; yet, if they get what they want, the chase is over. Guys need the chase. It's in their hardwired animal instincts. The more chase you give them, the more they are going to go crazy trying to catch you. If you give in right away, your chase was super easy and not worth pursuing anymore. They might not want to pursue you anyway if you sleep with them in the first couple of dates and they think you're like that with every other guy you meet.

I know we're not all virgins, and yes, we like having sex. I know I do. It's just natural and nothing to be ashamed of. I'm not saying you should completely be abstinent while you're single. I wouldn't ask anything of you that I wouldn't do myself, and this isn't an option for me. I would explode and rip the clothes off the next hot guy I went out with. Just keep the heavy petting to a minimum. You want the guy to love you for your mind, body, and soul—not just your moves in the bedroom. Plus, you want it to be special when you do enjoy each other. If he only wants you for sex without a relationship, then he'll tire after a few dates and give up.

When you're single and not looking for one-night stands, you definitely need to invest in some toys. There's no reason you have to completely deprive yourself if you're not in a relationship. Every human being has sexual urges. Otherwise, we would never reproduce. It's definitely safer and smarter to just take a visit to your local XXX store. If you feel uncomfortable, go online. There are plenty of places where you can find some good stuff and most of the time it ships in an unmarked box. So you don't have to worry about the mailman thinking you're kinky!

Hot and heavy make out sessions are totally okay in the beginning stages of dating. There's nothing wrong with that. Just be careful when or where you have them in case you can't control yourself. Don't do a first date or second date as an in-home meal/movie combo. That might be too easy to turn into a sleepover. It's better to go out to dinner and be somewhere in public. If you don't know your date that well, this is a good personal safety measure. I'll get more into safety in a later chapter.

If you keep getting unwanted advances and he won't back off, ditch him. He obviously doesn't respect you now, so why would he ever? He thinks that only his needs are important and not yours. Don't let yourself get into a predicament if he keeps coming onto you physically. If he won't lay off, just leave. Definitely do not put yourself in a situation where you are alone. Stay in public places.

Not everyone in this day and age is looking for a committed, serious relationship. Maybe you just got out of a serious relationship and you're just looking for a fun, no-strings-attached (NSA) situation. There's nothing wrong with that either. Just be open and honest with the other person so they don't get led on or hurt. They might be looking for more than you are, or vice versa. You would want the same from the other person you are hanging out with as well. Being up front and honest from the beginning ensures that no one's feelings get hurt.

Most of these NSA or friends with benefits (FWB) situations can be very beneficial to both parties. You just need to be safe and communicate with each other. Both of you lay out what your expectations are and don't expect more. Don't get into an emotional love affair. Take it for what it is at face value. If you're not able to keep emotions out of a sexual relationship, then it's probably not the situation for you. Be honest with yourself about what you want and can handle. Don't get in over your head. If you enter one of these situations and soon find out it's more than you can handle, just let the other person know as soon as possible; otherwise, you're going to be the one getting hurt.

Some people are into having an open relationship, where you have a special someone you're with all the time like a boyfriend/ girlfriend, husband/wife, yet you both agree to openly see other people. There's nothing wrong with this type of relationship, but both parties *must* agree to it. With approximately 50% of all marriages ending in divorce, I'm not here to judge what kind of relationship is best for you. Maybe more people should be having open relationships. Maybe that would make marriages last longer. I'm not really sure. What works for one couple may not work for another. The key to making any relationship work is keeping communication open and having the freedom to discuss issues. I think that's where most things crumble. It's fine to want a monogamous, NSA/FWB, or open relationship, just as long as both parties agree to the terms. It's not fair to start a relationship one way then one person decides it's going to change without discussing it with their partner. That would be cheating. No one likes to be cheated on. Just know what you want and what you can live with. If you can't handle an open relationship, then don't be with someone who wants that. Know what you want and don't settle for less.

On another aspect of respecting yourself: watch out for the person who's always changing your plans. Your date may have unexpected issues come up on short notice, which is understandable. But if they're always changing plans at the last minute so you have to rearrange your schedule, it's disrespectful. That person is not taking your time into consideration. For example, I had a very important appointment with a copy editor that took me two weeks to arrange. I had gone on one date with a guy and he asked me out again. He texted me and I told him I could meet him at 8 PM because I had an appointment at 5 PM. He said okay, but an hour later he asked if I could meet him at 6. I said no, I had a very important appointment. He texted me back and asked me to move my appointment so he could see me sooner. I responded that it was a very important meeting and there was no way in hell I was moving it for him. He obviously didn't care about me or my needs, or what was important to me. He only cared about himself and his needs.

Be wary of others who always want you to change your life for them. Your life is important, and there's no reason you can't both compromise. If you start changing all your plans to accommodate them, it will be like that forever. You mean nothing and everything revolves around them. Don't be with someone who is that selfish. You'll be miserable catering to their needs all the time. He'll be the sun and you'll just be another planet in orbit around him.

When you do state your boundaries and let them know when they have overstepped, pay attention to their reaction. Hopefully they will apologize and try to work with you on the situation. If they completely ignore your wishes or pretend like they care to only do it again, dismiss them because they're probably not a person who you want to be with. Two people need to give and take, you respect their boundaries/feelings and they respect yours. If you voice your opinion over and over again and they just don't get it, they probably never will. They are selfish and self-centered—pretty difficult characteristics to change in someone else. Don't waste your time. Find someone who cares enough to respect you, your boundaries and your feelings.

OVERVIEW: Rule #6

- Respect yourself and your boundaries.

- Don't have sex within the first couple of dates.

- Know what kind of relationship you want and communicate that to your partner.

RULE #7

STEER CLEAR OF ADDICTS

Alcoholics, drug addicts, or anyone with another sort of addiction problem should be avoided at all costs. You may not know the person you're dating is an alcoholic or drug addict at first. It won't be long until you find out, though. Relationships are hard enough on their own without the drama of an addictive personality thrown into the mix. The problem is they have a force greater than themselves they can't control. The addiction will always take precedence over everything, and you will always be second on the list. It will be a battle you cannot win.

If you become involved with someone who is an addict and you try to save them, you're adding the lost puppy syndrome to the problem. Obviously, they're not mature enough to take care of themselves or their problem. Your attempts to save them aren't going to make a healthy relationship either. No matter how hard you try or what you do to help them, they ultimately have to save themselves. If they decide they want to sober up and they do it for you, that will never work either. They have to have the desire to want to kick their habit for themselves. If you kick them out, they may go to rehab and clean up for a while to get you back. But they can very easily slip back into their old ways. I've seen many addicts do it over and over again —go into one expensive rehab clinic after another and sober up while they're there, just to go back to their old ways as soon as they return home.

When people are addicted to drugs or other substances, they are usually not themselves while under the influence. You may be dating someone who is constantly high, drunk, or on pain pills, and their personality is one way. They are happy, fun to be around, outgoing, or relaxed. You get used to being with that person and the way the drugs make them behave. Once they finally sober up, they can be a completely different person. Some may become sad, depressed, introverted, and angry. There are most likely a lot deeper issues going on beneath the surface and this is why they turned to drug use to ease the pain.

Once they are sober they have to face reality. They are going to have a hard road to ahead of them to travel. It's great they want to clean up their life, but now you don't recognize the person you've known all this time. It's like looking at a stranger. Who is this person? It's not the same person you knew or fell in love with, it's someone else. You fell in love with the addictive personality, not the clean and sober version.

I did my fair share of drugs in high school and then in college. I was trying to self-medicate my pain of a lost childhood, a difficult father, a brother who had lots of special needs, a mother who was emotionally unavailable, and other life issues. Sometimes it just seemed easier to get high or drunk to dull the pain instead of actually dealing with the issues. The problem is that the issues never go away, they just get shoved down further and further, but eventually they do surface. I pushed mine down until the age of 33. When they all came out it was like a geyser.

You're not going to be able to help this person; they have to be the ones to help themselves. Only when a person hits rock bottom can they then see they need to change once and for all. You can try to gently lead them in the right direction, but they have to be the ones to decide to change for themselves.

Some people never do change. They will be caught in a downward spiral for the rest of their lives. Don't let them pull you down with them. It's not your responsibility, it's theirs. Let them deal with their life.

I met my first fiancé when I lived in California at the ripe age of 23, right after graduating college. He was a piece of work: 32 years old, sous chef, alcoholic, drug addict with ADD and Type I diabetes. I think, in a sense, I was trying to save him from himself. I had quit drugs at the end of my freshman year of college. When I met my first fiancé he would dabble a little in weed, then it went onto ecstasy, then onto methamphetamines and always paired with alcohol. I do admit I did ecstasy with him twice. I hated it and it reminded me of why I quit all that stuff to begin with. So I tried to help him quit as well. Of course it didn't go over well. Most of our relationship involved me giving him insulin shots because he would get drunk, sleep in the morning, forget to do it himself and then go into a diabetic seizure. I kept candy in my car just in case his sugar levels would dip too low because he wouldn't eat. I even had to take him to the hospital once where he stayed for a few days because he almost slipped into a diabetic coma. That was the final straw. I told him I couldn't take care of him anymore, that he needed to go into rehab, and I couldn't deal with it. So he did, and it lasted about 3 months. He got sober during his stay. Once they released him, it was only about a week until he fell off the wagon. He locked himself in his bathroom with his dog and got high as Lucy in the sky with diamonds. That's when it was over for me. His addiction was a power that was too strong for either of us to handle. I couldn't waste my time trying to save him anymore. He had to save himself. I hope he did eventually clean himself up.

If you are already in a relationship with an addict, you know what a struggle it is. For the most part, it's like taking care of a child. They can't do much for themselves or really have any responsibility. You're the only adult in the situation. Having to take care of them involves all aspects: financial, physical, and emotional. It's a lot of stress for a relationship. If you get married and have kids, they're just going to weigh you down with responsibility even more. They are already the kid in the relationship. I would strongly suggest rethinking your relationship if you are in one with an addict. Maybe they have cleaned themselves up, maybe they are trying to. If it's stressing your relationship to the point where you are losing yourself, it may not be the best thing to stay in it for the long haul. Only you can decide what's best for you.

OVERVIEW: Rule #7

- Steer clear of addicts; once you discover someone is, get out.

- Don't try to save an addict; it's a power greater than you or them.

RULE #8

HAVE FUN, BE YOURSELF & DON'T LOSE YOUR IDENTITY

When you're out in the dating jungle, it's important to be yourself. Remember, it's fun going out there and meeting new people. Relax, enjoy it and have fun. Don't try to put on a show and pretend to be someone else. That never works. Eventually the truth will come out, and if they like the person you're trying to be, they may not like the real you. You want someone to like you for *you*. Otherwise, how can you have a long-term relationship with them?

Before you go out on a date, don't let your anxiety get the best of you. It's scary and nerve-wracking meeting someone new for the first time. If you are the kind of person that's shy or gets super nervous around new people, try some of these techniques before you meet up with your date. About 10 minutes before you leave your house (I do this while I'm doing my hair and makeup), start positive self-talk. Look yourself in the mirror and say positive things while taking deep, relaxing breaths. Examples are:

1) I matter

2) I'm a loving and caring human being

3) I'm ready to accept love into my life

4) I'm ready for a healthy relationship

5) I deserve to be happy

6) I'm a smart and educated person

7) I'm confident and courageous

8) I'm an intelligent and beautiful person

Make sure the little voices in your head are filled with positive, self-affirming talk. If anything negative comes into your mind, quickly replace it with something positive. Say one of the self-affirmations listed above. Say it out loud while looking at yourself in the mirror. Scream it if you have to! Nothing is a bigger turn-off than going out with a negative person. By cleansing your attitude with positive self-talk, you will be cleansing your aura. You will glow with positive energy, which attracts other people with positive energy. Energy types definitely pull towards each other. Ever notice how happy people tend to be with other happy people and negative people gravitate towards other negative people? You will attract similar types of people with the energy that you are putting out there in the world. Make sure you are putting out positive vibes!

Now you're ready to meet your date. Once you meet up, be sure to make eye contact when you first see them. You want to come off as a confident person. When you're sitting down for dinner, drinks, coffee, or whatever you decided on, make sure to be attentive, sitting up straight and focusing on them. Don't focus on the pretty girl over at the next table or the hot waiter . . that's really annoying. Not making and maintaining eye contact will subconsciously tell your date that they don't matter. Make sure your date has your complete and undivided attention. Even if you decide within the first 10 minutes this isn't the person for you, there's still no reason to be rude. You don't want to burn your bridges. If there's no romantic connection, you can always make a good friend. No one can ever have too many friends. You never know, this person may have connections to that Fortune 500 company you've been trying to land a job at for the last 5 years. Always be a courteous person. You would want the same done to you.

Discussion topics on the first few dates should be light and airy. You want to get to know the other person, but you need to not get into really intense topics. Most people feel very strongly in their beliefs. If you say something to offend them, you are going to put them off from the very beginning. They may not be able to see past that and take the time to get to know you. Neutral topics are the best things to discuss to keep you from treading on thin ice. Also, check your baggage at the door. Don't go into the details of your nasty divorce and how evil your ex is over appetizers. Don't dish all the gossip about your crazy family before you finish your first drink. Give your date ample time to get to know who you are *before* you unload all your baggage on them. It's too much information in the beginning, and they won't be able to look past the drama to see who you really are. Make sure they're someone you want to share the intimate details of your life with as well. Don't just share all your secrets with everyone, save them for the people you hold close to your heart.

Good Topics for First Dates:	Bad Topics for First Dates:
1) Sports 2) Travels 3) Music 4) Food 5) Hobbies 6) Movies/Books 7) Your Job 8) Where you went to school and grew up 9) Kids if you have them (but don't dominate the conversation with them)	1) Religion (unless it's super important you date within your own religion) 2) Politics (unless it's important to you) 3) Your crazy ex 4) How many times you've been married or engaged 5) All your family's deep dark secrets 6) That time you didn't pay your taxes 7) When you lost your virginity the first time 8) How far in debt you are in 9) What drugs you have experimented with

While you're having these first date conversations, also try to see if they have the qualities that you want in a partner. You need to know what's important to you in another person. Write down a list of 5-7 traits that you must have in a partner—any characteristic that is non-negotiable to you. Never more than 7, nobody is going to be perfect. The perfect person that has all your qualities is a fantasy. Get out of the fantasy and back into reality. If you have a list of 20 things, no one will fill all those besides a blow-up doll. You will have to compromise on a few things. Write your 5 non-negotiable qualities and keep it as a mental note every time you go out on a date.

Example of a Quality List:

1) Ambitious attitude
2) Likes to travel, especially abroad
3) Works out and eats healthy
4) Spiritual
5) Loving, caring and attentive
6) Positive outlook on life
7) Accepting of all races and nationalities

Your list may look completely different than this, and there's nothing wrong with that. Just think of the qualities that you want most in a mate. Think long term, someone you could spend the rest of your life with. It doesn't matter exactly what they are, as long as they are important to you. I'm not really into politics much, but some people are totally involved in it; either they work in politics or it's just an aspect that they feel deeply about. If you are a Liberal and could never identify with a Republican's point of view, then a relationship with two people of such opposite points of view probably wouldn't work out. It may be okay in the beginning, but down the road you're going to have lots of arguments that will cause tension in the relationship. If one person is strongly political and the other isn't so much, then it's most likely not a big deal. The easy-going person isn't going to make a big deal of topics at hand so it won't cause big problems.

Know what's important to you, your values, and your beliefs. I know it's hard to narrow it down to just a few qualities. If you're having a hard time with that, start off big. Write down every quality you want. Then pare it down by half, then another half, and another, until you have about 5 core qualities.

Compiling your list will also make you aware of the core qualities within yourself. Don't change yourself to fit the mold of someone else. Say the person you are dating regularly attends Sunday mass, is vegetarian, and loves to volunteer at the homeless shelter. Your concept of worship is going only on holidays, you love yourself a big juicy steak, and your idea of charity is more like giving your old Coach purse to your little cousin. You probably won't be a good match. Don't change yourself just to "be the person" your date wants. In the beginning you think you can give up meat only 'til 6 months later when you're downing a cheeseburger in the drive-thru on your lunch break. Be who you are and be happy about it. Shout it to the world! You'll be able to find someone who loves you for you. It's exhausting trying to pretend to be someone you're not.

Some people are so eager to change for someone else. It will never work out in the long run. If you've been in a long-term relationship and are just now getting out of it, you may not even know who you are yet. If you've spent your entire relationship trying to make the other person happy to no avail, you may need some time to get to know *you* again. It's just like Julia Roberts in *Runaway Bride*. She had been with a man her entire life and continually adapted to each of her partner's persona—and each one was very different. She spent so much time trying to become something that the other wanted; she didn't even know what she wanted any more. She didn't even know how she liked her eggs cooked. Don't be the runaway bride. Know yourself. Take the time to figure out who you really are. Healthy relationships can only come from two independent adults coming together. You can be together and not lose your identity. You partner should love you for you and all your qualities, inside and out.

OVERVIEW: Rule #8

- Have fun, relax, and say your affirmations before going on a date.

- Stick to light topics in conversation.

- Write down your 5 non-negotiables and remember them during each date.

- Don't lose your identity!

RULE #9

BE SAFE, RESEARCH YOUR DATES

Protecting Yourself and Your Information

In this day and age of meeting people over the internet, with chat rooms and all other methods, you need to make sure to be safe. Even if you met a guy/girl in person at a bar, you never know who they really are. When you set up dates make sure to both drive your own car and meet somewhere public. Tell one of your friends where you're going and the name of your date. Never meet anyone at their house or yours. You don't want them knowing where you live just in case the date goes bad and you never want to see them again. It's best to keep meeting in public places until the third date or so, just to make sure you think you know the other person well enough to come and pick you up.

When meeting someone online, don't give out your phone number right away. If someone asks for your phone number after a few conversations, give them your email address first. I would recommend creating an email that you will use just for dating purposes. Do not give out your work email because (a) it's not professional, and (b) that person will know exactly where you work. Not smart things to do with someone you do not know very well. If things go wrong, they may start stalking you at your work. (Example: I dated this guy for a month or so and he had my work email. When I decided he wasn't the one for me, he got very upset and subscribed my work email to all kinds of pornographic websites. I was bombarded during the day with thousands of nasty emails. I finally had to tell my boss and the company had to delete that email account and create me an entirely new one. Not particularly a fun thing to tell your boss.)

Don't give out a personal email that you use in Facebook, forums, or any other online uses either. If you Google the email address you use to log into Facebook it will pull up your Facebook page. If you do not have your Facebook profile set to private, this person will be able to see all your photos, all your friends and family members, and any other important information you have in there. God forbid you have your home address listed. Bam! This stranger you never met now knows exactly where you live. It's kinda scary, the information a complete stranger can pull up on you. You have to be internet-smart. If you do use social media I suggest making your pages private. Facebook tends to change its privacy settings frequently, so make sure to keep it up to date. I have mine set to completely private so even if someone does find my page, they can only see my profile photo, nothing else. The best thing to do is create a Yahoo or Gmail account to be used strictly for dating purposes. When creating this account, use your real first name, but do not put your entire last name. For example, I would name mine *Tara R*. That way when you email them, they will not know your full last name, so they can't search my full name either. They will find out your full name in time if they prove themselves worthy.

Finding Out if Your Date is Safe

Making sure that your potential date is not a serial killer might seem a little overboard, but in this day and age, it's better to be safe than sorry. You know how easy it is to find information on someone over the internet, so utilize it. There are lots of free resources online, depending upon what counties you live in, just Google certain items. In most counties you can search criminal files and the jail databases. It's all public information to find out who's in jail and what crime they are being held for. Most databases will be able to tell you the arrest record on a certain individual for up to 15 years online for free. It will list their name, date of birth, crime and mug shot so you know if it's the same person. You can also search for registered sex offenders. All sex offenders must register wherever they live and you can even search by someone's email address. Of course, email addresses are easy to create, but it doesn't hurt to try. Since you can't necessarily ask someone for their social or driver's license number, use all the info you can. Even just Googling someone's name brings up a plethora of information. Just make sure it's on the right person. There are lots of similar names out there.

For example, if you wanted to search criminal records for Hillsborough County in Tampa, you would Google *Hillsborough County Sheriff Dept*. Click the Arrest Inquiry and it presents a search box. All you have to enter is Last Name, First Name, Race, and Sex, then you'll be given the arrest records. Most searches go a few years back. Hillsborough Sheriff's office has records online for 16 years. You may have to search multiple counties if you live somewhere where there are a lot of adjacent counties. If you know your date has just moved from a different area, get the name of the county or state and search there as well. Don't be too obvious, like asking, "Oh, what was the name of the county you lived in?" Just find out the city and remember it, then you can Google it later the next day to find out what county it is. Most county-level searches are free.

If you want to do a statewide criminal search, depending upon your state's laws, you may have to pay for it. Make sure you have the most accurate information on the person you want to search: full name, birthdate, race, sex, height, weight, eye color, and hair color. You do not want to pay for inaccurate records. You can do the statewide criminal searches through government websites as well. I trust these over other sites that basically pull the same information from them and might cost you more. Arrest records are public in most states, though some people can order to have their records sealed or expunged. This means that you would not be able to find their records even if they had been arrested or convicted of a crime. Keep in mind that even if no records come back in these searches, they will still charge you the fees.

The National Sex Offender database (http://www.familywatchdog.us) is free, and you can search by state or name. You can also search the entire US for the same name. This is helpful for more than just dating purposes. It helps keeps track of sex offenders who move into your neighborhood if you have children.

If you want to find out if someone is married, divorced, or other domestic records, that can be found in your county's Clerk of Court office. All this is public information as well. Each county is different on how to search the records. Most counties should have a searchable database online. Just Google *Clerk of Court Records (your county)*. For example, Hillsborough

County records go back to 1965, that's a pretty decent time frame. Sometimes in the search field it works best to just use the last name. Most marriage and divorce records have a person's middle name recorded, so if you don't know their entire name and search by just the first and last name, it may not pull up anything. Just search by the person's last name and you will get more results to filter through. Now remember, if you are searching for women within the marriage documents, the marriage certificate will show up under her maiden name. Just keep that into consideration. For men it's easier, since they do not change their last name.

Be wary of those online background checks that promote finding information from just someone's name. There are a lot of people with the same name out there. I've already done searches on myself and there's way more Tara Richters out there in the world than I would have hoped for! You need to make sure you are getting the correct information on the correct person. You don't want to pay $100 just to find random info on the wrong person. It's better to be more specific, such as the county of residence or birth date, so you can narrow it down. Don't go too crazy or overboard, either. Just do a few checks to make sure this person is who they say they are. If you start getting the feeling that something wishy-washy is going on, you're probably right. Trust your instincts.

Just Googling someone's name can pull up a vast array of items. LinkedIn.com and CorporationWiki.com is an easy way to find out someone's executive profiles to see if they really do have the job or work for the company they say they do. Doing simple checks like this, just to see if their stories jive, is never a bad idea. Keep in mind, like I said before, that there are people out there with the same name. For example, if I Google Tara Richter, I apparently am a photographer for Richter Photography, a graduate of Hononegah High School in Rockton, IL, a teacher in Greenville County, and also a graduate of Richland Center High School in Richland Center, WI. This is all on the first page of results. None of these are actually me.

Example: This Actually Happened to Me

I met a guy on a dating website. We conversed through email and a few text messages for about a week. His profile said he lived in Orlando, but when I asked, he said he didn't really have a place he called home. He traveled all the time for work. Though he used to live in Illinois, goes to London for work, but right now is living out of hotel rooms. That sounded a little fishy, but I know some people travel a lot for business. He said he was a coach, mentor and does speaking engagements. He wanted me to go to Orlando for a date and said he wanted to take me shopping at the Outlet Mall. Well, what girl would turn that down? So we planned on a date for the following week. He cancelled a few days later and said he had to go back to London to fill in for a friend at the last minute. I asked what he did in London for work, he said he takes people to watch soccer games. That sounded weird to me, too. Why do you need to take them to watch soccer? Can't they just go themselves? He wanted to reschedule our date for the following week.

I decided to do some research on this guy. Before I drove all the way to Orlando and back (which is a 3 hour round trip for me) I needed to find out more details. He had not given me a lot of info about him, he was always asking questions about me. He asked me if I was married. I told him I was divorced, yet I asked him the same and he didn't respond, instead he changed the subject. Also, another weird thing was that he would never call me. It's been my experience that if a guy never calls you, or only does during the day then goes MIA at night, it's because he's married. It's easier for him to text you in front of his wife than call you.

I had his full name and business email address. I Googled it and found his LinkedIn.com profile. On his profile it had his personal and business websites. I went to those and discovered he had opened a Great Clips. It had photos of him, a woman and a child on that site. So, I'm assuming he's married with a child. It had her name, Lisa, within the captions of the photos, but nothing more. I went back to LinkedIn.com and his profile stated that his business served the greater Chicago, IL area. I went to WhitePages.com and searched him in Chicago. It actually pulled up that he lived right outside in a small town in Wisconsin. Though, on WhitePages.com it will tell you the address, who else is living within that household and the approximate age range. The name of the woman in the photos matched the information within WhitePages.com. I wanted to see if I could pull up their marriage certificate, even though for me this was evidence enough that he was a married man. I searched their address to find the county they resided in. It came up as Kenosah. I went to the Kenosah County Clerk of Courts website. Unfortunately, Kenosah makes you pay to search family records. I didn't want to cough up the money, so instead I searched the Kenosah Circuit Court Records. I discovered that their house went into foreclosure at the beginning of the year with his wife's name on the docket. Also, he was sued for an automobile/injury accident back in 1993. Right there, the proof is in the pudding. He's married, without even needing to search the family courts. If her name is on the foreclosure docket, then it had to of been on the title, mortgage and/or deed. Normally you wouldn't have someone on the title, etc. unless it's a spouse or in other cases a sibling/parent. I didn't believe the latter to be the case. Especially since I saw their family portrait on the Great Clips website.

I decided I would let this man know that I discovered he was married. I didn't want to send an email simply asking if he was because he could say things like *"Oh, we're separated,"* yadda yadda. I wanted him to know that I knew everything about him without threatening him, just to make him shake in his boots a little. I sent him a short email. All it said was, "So, how is Lisa doing?" I never heard back.

Within 10 minutes I discovered all this information on a man I was conversing with over the internet. Thank goodness for public records! It's so easy in this day and age to find out if someone is full of crap or telling you the truth. The internet is a great tool to find information and most of it is for FREE. You need to take responsibility for who you are dating. Don't leave it up to them. You don't want to get involved in a relationship and then 2 months down the line have some woman come knocking on your door. It's just like defensive driving. It would be nice to think everyone's a good driver, but they're not. The roads are filled with crazy drivers that do stupid things like pull out in front of you. You have to maneuver around them, slam on your breaks and swerve out of the way to avoid getting your car smashed. The same goes for dating— practice safe dating. Be smart, do your research, it will save you a lot of grief down the road!

OVERVIEW: Rule #9

- Protect your information; don't put everything out on the internet for strangers to find.

- Do online searches to see if your date is safe and they are who they say they are.

- Meet in public places for the first few dates.

RULE #10

TRY NEW PLACES & BE MORE APPROACHABLE

Try New Places

Do you find yourself stuck in a rut? Are you on all kinds of different dating websites, yet keep finding the same duds? Are you going out to the bars but only find bimbos? You may be stuck in a dating rut, doing the same things over and over again expecting different results—the definition of insanity. I know it's hard going out there and trying to meet new people for the first time in years. I'm in the same boat as all of you reading my book. If you think you're in a dating rut and not meeting the kinds of people you want to, then you need to try new places.

It's easy meeting new people when you're young, in school and starting new jobs. Then you get older and everyone's married. All of a sudden it's really hard meeting new people. Start by thinking of hobbies or things you like to do. Do you like working out, reading books, drinking wine? Anything you like doing, make a list. Write down all of your hobbies and anything you like to do for fun. Once you have your list, start Googling local clubs in your area that have outings or anything to do with your hobby. Say you love to read books. Find out if there's a local book club in your area. Or maybe you love riding bikes. There's lots of weekend biking clubs. Maybe you're into wines. You like drinking wine, so instead of going to the bars, you could enroll in a community college class for wine tasting. It would be a fun environment to educate yourself and meet other people who are also interested in learning about wine culture.

Here's a list of new things to try to get yourself out of the dating rut and meeting new people, maybe finding some fun new hobbies in the process!

1) Tennis lessons

2) Golf lessons

3) Biking groups

4) Kayaking

5) Learn a new language at your local community college

6) Take a cooking class or go to one of those places where you can cook meals for a week with other people, e.g. Dinner My Way

7) Go on a singles cruise

8) Take a wine tasting class

9) Go speed dating

10) Sign up for a gym if you aren't already and participate in the classes, e.g. yoga, zumba, spinning, kickboxing, et cetera. That setting is easier to talk to people than just walking around a gym.

11) "It's Just Lunch," a company that matches up young professionals on a group date lunch environment. Google the name to find a local establishment by you.

12) Baseball or football game (great place for women to meet guys).

13) "Events and Adventures" (a company that organizes events specifically for single people. It's kind of expensive, but might be worth it depending upon your budget.)

14) Anything else you've been dying to do in your life!

The thing to remember is that this is a new chapter in your life. Start trying new things! It's fun, you'll meet new people—if not a soul mate, then at least some new friends along the way. Don't get stuck surfing the internet in your condo for dates all by yourself and your cat. Get out there! Do something! This is your chance to turn your life around. If you've just gone through a bad divorce, or even if it was a mutual breakup, now is not the time to jump on the pity wagon. Think about all the fun stuff you now get to do because you're single! It really helped me to think of all the positive stuff I was able to do after my divorce. Even little stuff like watching hours of *Keeping up with the Kardashians* without anyone nagging at me. I know it's awful, but my guilty pleasure is watching reality TV. Lou hated it and always had control of the remote. Can you believe I went 4 years without smut tv?! I'm surprised I didn't go crazy . . . or maybe that's what made me go crazy!

The point is, have fun. Don't pressure yourself too much. Don't say, "OMG I'm 45 and single for the first time in 20 years. I'll never find anyone. I'll be alone for the rest of my life; I must marry the first man/woman I meet!" Stop with any negative self-talk. This is your chance to take back your life! Think of anything and everything you've wanted to do with your life and didn't because you were in a relationship or your wife/husband wouldn't like it. Well, now you're single! Go out there and do all the crazy stuff you've always wanted to. I personally give you permission. Just don't go skydiving without a parachute or something stupid like that.

For me, going through a divorce when I never ever wanted to divorce in my life has opened up new doors. My life has taken a left-hand turn that wasn't in my internal GPS. At first I was upset and unaccepting. Now that I'm moving on, though, I see it all happened for a reason. I am fulfilling my lifelong dreams of writing books, going back to school for hypnotherapy, and becoming a life coach. I never would have realized my dreams if not for this tragedy that really was a blessing in disguise. It also made me look more into myself from an outside point of view and made me realize why I do the things I do. You cannot make changes in your life unless you can look outside yourself. It was almost as if I had been looking at life through a shattered window my entire life. Now I've fixed the window and can see everything clearly. Seize the opportunity that life has given you. I know some days it's tough to be positive, but just keep doing your affirmations and it will pull you through. Or go eat a little chocolate cake . . . that always helps too!

Be More Approachable

When you go out trying to meet new people, it's very intimidating for men and women alike. No one likes rejection. I honestly think the older you get, the harder it is to approach people out in public. You don't know if someone is married, engaged, attached, or just plain nuts. When you're younger, most of the time you know someone is most likely not married. I know some marry young, but for the most part everyone in college is single or dating.

I used to have a rule that I would never go up and approach a guy, me being the woman. That used to work when I was in my twenties. My friends and I had more guys hitting on us than we knew what to do with. Now, being single again at 33, things are a little different. Guys are not as outgoing and do not approach us as much. Granted, I've been told I'm fairly attractive, so I didn't understand why nobody asked me out. I've also been told in person that I look about 25 when I'm actually 33, which is a bonus. But men are still apprehensive about approaching me. I will be at a bar and notice a guy will be staring at me from across it for an hour or more without actually walking over and saying anything. As I've taken more notice to the behaviors of others around me, I find a lot of men doing this. I once had a guy at the gym tell me that I always look like I'm angry. He had been wanting to approach me but didn't know how because I didn't look approachable at all. I had no idea I was doing this. I just usually have a lot on my mind and am in thought most of the time. It doesn't matter how hot you are; if you come off as unapproachable, no one will feel comfortable striking up conversations with you. They don't want to be rejected. I'm actually a really nice person once you speak to me and get to know me. I had no idea I was throwing off this unapproachable vibe.

I consciously have been making an effort to smile more and say hi to random strangers out and about. Just saying "Hi" to someone can open a whole world of opportunities. There doesn't need to be any crazy/cheesy pickup lines. One small word opens the door to communication. Most women don't want the cheesy pick-up lines anyway. We just want a normal guy to have a conversation with. So remember to smile and let your walls down. If you continuously live in a guarded world, no one is going to want to strike up conversation. Make yourself more approachable. Smiling makes a world of difference.

Once I started applying this when I was out with friends, guys started approaching me more and I actually started approaching them. I understand how a guy doesn't want to be rejected and women feel exactly the same way. Yes, I have been rejected after approaching a guy. It sucked, but oh well, I just took my drink and walked over to the other bar. If you never put yourself out there, you always are going to miss out on meeting new people and opportunities. But at least you can say you tried. Get yourself out of your comfort zone. I used to be a die-hard believer that a woman should never approach a guy. Well, now I have thrown that idea out the window. If I notice a guy staring at me for a long period of time from across the bar, I either go talk to him or I give him a wave to come over and talk to me. All you need is that one small ice breaker to open the conversation. All I ever say in the first line is "Hi." It's so simple, yet so complex. This is how the guy I met in my gym started conversation with me. I walked in, saw him, and said "Hi." Then he came over and talked to me after his workout. Then the next time we talked during our entire workout for about an hour.

So girls, if you're going out and wondering why guys are not approaching you, it's okay to approach them. I would start off with a little flirting first. Definitely have some eye contact. Don't just randomly go up to the first hot guy you see. Scope out the scene; see who's around and who's making eye contact with you. If you repeatedly try to make eye contact with a guy and he doesn't reciprocate, move on. Don't approach him, he's obviously not interested and you will most likely get rejected. Same goes for the guys. If a girl doesn't make eye contact, it's probably a no-go.

Establishing eye contact from across the room, the table, or the bar with someone you want to meet is basically a non-verbal invitation. If you consistently make eye contact, without staring and looking like a stalker, you pretty much have been given the green light to initiate conversation. Then it's up to one of the parties to actually initiate. I would say after 5 to 10 minutes of eye contact flirting, you're safe to go on to an actual conversation and your chances of getting shot down are pretty slim to none. They must like you if they keep looking at you.

If you're not comfortable with the eye contact flirting, practice it. Just like any good athlete, you need to practice your skills. I used to do this a lot when I was in high school and college. Everywhere I went, I would practice eye contact. It's just pure, innocent fun. If you're shy, this is a very good skill for you to work on. I know from being super shy myself when I was in grade school, it's hard making and establishing eye contact. It's something that you can definitely work your way out of. Try it out wherever you go: the mall, grocery shopping, eating dinner, or the gym. As you walk down the grocery store aisle, pick a person and, as you gradually walk closer to them, look them in the eyes. Don't stare—make eye contact for only a couple seconds, anything longer seems creepy. See if they return the eye contact. If they don't it's okay, either try again or move on to someone else. If they do return the eye contact, then hold it a couple seconds longer with a smile. If you don't smile, you are going to come off as a creepy stalker. You wouldn't want someone looking at you with an angry look, would you? If they return the eye contact with a smile as well, and by this time you're probably fairly close in proximity to this person, give them a compliment. Say you like their outfit, shoes, tattoo, whatever. Something simple. Nothing weird or sexual like, "I like your ass." Even complimenting their face or body would be weird. Though you could say, "I love your hairdo," if you can tell they had it professionally done. You can even practice this with the same sex. This might be easier for women complimenting women, but guys can too. Maybe you like their car or motorcycle. It doesn't have to be weird. Guys can compliment other guys.

A lot of people will like something another person is wearing or whatnot, but they won't actually *say* it to that person because they don't know them. People really need to get over this. I would rather have someone stare at me and say they love my purse instead of just staring. I would have no idea why! Do I have a booger in my nose? Is my skirt stuck in my underwear? People really need to start giving out more compliments to strangers. It makes you feel good, they feel good, and you just opened up a line of communication. You would be surprised how chatty strangers can become when you give them one simple little compliment. Start making eye contact and complimenting people, and break out of your shell! It's the only way you're going to meet new people. Doing just these two simple things will make you a lot more approachable to guys and girls alike. Start off by giving a random stranger a compliment once a day. It's amazing how good it makes you feel to know you brightened someone else's day. You can do it to people you don't feel threatened by, like the elderly woman who lives down the street. Do it until you feel comfortable saying it to the hot girl next door.

Before you make that compliment, though, take the ear buds out of your head. A big way to make yourself more approachable is to not walk around listening to your iPod or talking on your Bluetooth headset. I know this is the high-tech age and I love my iPhone as much as the next person, but don't walk around listening to your iPod unless you're at the gym working out. Now a days you see people walking around with headphones on all the time. It used to be just the gym. Now it's walking, on the bus, at Starbucks, and the mall. How are you supposed to approach someone who's wearing headphones? Even if you just wanted to say "Hi," they most likely will not hear you. No one is even going to ask you for directions because it looks like you don't want to be bothered. Maybe you don't. It's fine to be in peace by yourself sometimes, but not all the time. If you live within isolation, you will be alone.

Technology has made us isolated and, in a way, is inhibiting our social skills. Instead of going outside the confines of our walls, we are retracting inside and using social media to take place of old-school socializing. As we stop going outside of our houses we forget how to socialize. For people who are shy, it may seem that internet dating is a blessing, but it can also be a curse. The more you get out there and practice interacting with people, the more comfortable you will be with it. You cannot live within the confines of your house and hide behind your computer screen forever. Eventually you will have to go out there and meet the person you are chatting with via Instant Messenger. Utilize the technology to your advantage, but do not become imprisoned within it.

If you have a hard time talking to strangers, go out with a friend who is a social butterfly. I myself sometimes don't like approaching strangers. Anyone who knows me knows I'm not into sports at all, although a great way to meet guys is by going to the local sports bar when the games are on. Approaching men in their natural environment makes them feel more comfortable. For instance, my roommate is a huge football fan and knows everything about all the teams and stats and I know diddly squat in that area. We will go to the nice bar/restaurant at the golf course by us (higher quality men hang out there versus a sleazy bar). She just starts talking to guys about this play, that team, this score, yadda yadda, whatever. Since she can connect with them on that level, it piques their interest and they start talking to both of us. She just broke the ice for all of us and I didn't even have to pay attention to the game. Hanging out with friends can help you meet people and break the ice for you.

OVERVIEW: Rule #10

- Get yourself out of the dating rut; try new places and new things.

- Practice your flirting skills.

- Make yourself more approachable.

- Don't be afraid to just say "Hi", men and women alike.

SUMMARY

Heal all of your wounds before you go out and start dating again. It doesn't matter if they come from a past divorce, traumatic childhood, or an old romance. You are damaged goods and will not be able to see things clearly until you heal yourself. Take all the time you need and possibly go to therapy if you think you need outside help.

Do not get involved with anyone who is still legally married to someone else. If you are the one just getting separated, wait until you have cleared up all your legal issues. Then wait anywhere between 6-12 months to start dating again. Take time to get back to you. Realize who you are before jumping back into another serious committed relationship. Have some time to yourself to have fun and be with friends and family who care about you. Don't just jump from one relationship to another.

Keep a mental note of repeat negative behaviors. After three instances of the same offense, they're out! Remember this with friends, co-workers, and family members as well. If you're confused about a certain person and not sure if they are good for you, write a list of good and bad qualities. See which list outweighs the other. If there are any signs of physical or verbal abuse, get out ASAP!

Avoid the knight in shining armor to come and save you. No one can save you from a bad situation, you have to save yourself. Watch out for peoples' actions and be wary of someone who talks a good game. Anyone can tell you how wonderful they are, but their actions will show you who they really are. Get your head out of the fantasy world and back to reality. If you feel yourself slipping into la la land, give yourself a reality check every now and then. Look at your situation from an outsider's point of view and detach yourself for just a bit. Is it as great as it seems to be?

Find someone who is your equal. Do not take in the needy people as significant others. Date within an acceptable age range. No more than 10 years younger or older than yourself. Find someone who is on a similar intelligence level as you. Two people who have the same sense of humor will go a long way!

Respect yourself and your boundaries. You know when someone is pushing your boundaries because it makes you feel uncomfortable. Put your foot down and don't let them take advantage of you. Decide what kind of relationship you do want and are comfortable with. Abstain from sex with your significant other until you know what kind of relationship the both of you want and agree to it.

Steer clear of addicts. Don't try to save an addict; their addiction is more powerful than you and them. Once you discover someone is an addict, it's best to let them clean up their act alone. Don't let them pull you into their downward spiral.

Remember to have fun, relax and be yourself when going out on dates. Say your affirmations while getting ready to cleanse your mind and attitude. Stick to light and airy topics in the beginning. You don't want to get into a political debate on the first date; it will turn the other person off. Decide what your 5 non-negotiable qualities in another person are. Don't lose your identity and try to be the person you think your date wants you to be. Find someone who loves you for you, flaws and all!

Be safe when you meet dates in person. Go somewhere public and drive your own car. Tell at least one person where you are going and who you are going to be with. If you meet someone at bar and they want you to go somewhere else in their car with them, get some identification from them. (My girlfriend snaps a photo of their driver's license on her iPhone, then texts it to a friend. That is really smart.) You never know in this day and age what people are up to. You can never be too safe. Do online searches if you're meeting someone from the internet. There are lots of free county websites to find out anyone's past record. Protect your information as well. Do not post all your information on social media sites. Leave off your home address, phone number, and college class schedule from Facebook. It's too easy to crack. Set your Facebook profile to private as well so it will not pop up in search engines.

Get yourself out of the dating rut. Try going to new places and doing new things. Enjoy being single and this part of your life. Realize that every new chapter is a time to experience new things. Get out there and find new hobbies. Practice your flirting skills. Do it every day for fun. Pay attention if someone's trying to flirt with you. The more you practice, the more you will catch on when someone is trying to catch your eye. Be confident inside. Make yourself more approachable by smiling to strangers, saying hi to neighbors and not paying more attention to your iPod than the human beings around you.

Once you utilize all the rules to find someone, focus all your energy on that one person. It's hard to get to know more than one person at a time. If you're dating multiple people you may not know who is making you feel what way. Date one person. Then listen to your heart. Pay close attention to how that person makes you feel inside. Do you get happy and giddy after a phone conversation with them, or do you feel sad and depressed? Do they make you second-guess your own judgment and decisions, or do they support you in your goals and career? If someone is constantly making you feel bad about yourself, they are not a healthy person. They need to go back and do Rule #1. You already have, so no need to wait around for them. Find the person that makes you feel great about being you! You are the only one who can find your lifelong love and happiness.

FINAL THOUGHTS

I'm happy to say that we've come to the end of the book. This wasn't any easy task for me to do, even though I've wanted to write books my entire life. I had all kinds of insecurities that would paralyze me from writing, like what my family would think of me if they read this or whether or not they would disown me. Plus, re-opening all my wounds and putting them in black and white for the world to see. Sometimes I would cry, not write for a couple of days, go back, then cry some more. Though, in a way, it was helping me accomplish Rule #1. By doing this I, in turn, healed my wounds. Within 6 months I completely turned my life around. I went from being miserable, doing what everyone else wanted me to do with my life, to doing what I wanted to do for me. Everyone told me I was crazy, that I wouldn't be able to do it. That's what really sets off the fire inside me. Such as when my father told me I could never make money doing what I loved, that I would have to be in real estate and work for him to make a living. That lit the fire inside me like coals on a freight train. I was on the track going full speed ahead. I was going to accomplish my goals and make something of myself just to prove him wrong.

You should never let other people dictate your life. That's what I did for 33 years. Letting the chatter of other people get into my head and tell me how to live my life. My mother was always telling me to just get a 9-5 job like every other "normal" person. My father was always telling me I had to work for him. Lou wanted me to get any job to pay bills, and be a household maid and sex goddess on top of it. When you're spending all this time pleasing other people and pushing your needs off to the side, you will never be happy. I couldn't give in and just have a 9-5 job, that's not me. I'm an entrepreneur. I worked in the corporate world for 10 years and I hated every minute of it. I got fired from more than half of the jobs I did have. I don't follow directions well and I didn't want to follow in someone else's footsteps. I wanted to pave my own path! That's what makes me excited and happy to live life, to keep conquering new obstacles and goals and do what others are not. Being a peg in a corporate wheel, spinning around and around doing the same thing day in and day out was killing my creative juices and the spark of life within me.

No one ever really understood who I was or what I wanted out of life. What made it worse is that I kept listing to everyone else besides myself. I didn't believe in myself either. I was stuck and miserable. I made a few attempts here and there at running my own businesses, but then would fail. I would let the chatter of other people get into my head. I would feel I needed to be like everyone else and just go get a "normal" job. I would do that for about a year, and then become even more miserable.

I was also letting this chatter mess with my head about relationships. When I met a guy the first things I would start to think are, *will my parents like him? Will he fit in with my friends? Will he be able to have a conversation with the entire family at Christmas dinner?* I was so worried about what everyone else would be thinking, I wasn't taking the time to see if we were compatible. I never asked myself, *do I like this guy?* It doesn't matter what anyone else thinks of the person you're with. The most important part is do they make you happy? It's hard to shut out the chatter of friends and family, but that's what you have to do. This is your life; they are not living it for you. They are not going to be there with that person through thick and thin. You are.

You have to own your life, live it without caring about what everyone else thinks, says or wants for you. Then you will free yourself to do whatever makes you happy! When you're happy you will attract other happy, strong, secure people. Within 6 months; I wrote and self-published this book, got my life coaching certificate, started my own business and sold my very first piece of artwork. 75% of the people I told what I was doing didn't believe in me. They told me I was crazy, which I probably am. Some of my friends didn't believe in me; my family always thinks I'm nuts. But I had a master plan. No one fully understood the complexity of my plan but me. This time I shut out all the chatter of everyone else. When someone would say something negative about my plan, I would turn a deaf ear. I kept telling myself, "It's ok, you can't blame them, they don't have the creative outlook like I do to fully understand." That right there was the only thing that kept me driving towards my goals. Even if I was the only one who believed in me, that was the only person I needed.

I kept applying the rules to every aspect in my life, not just to dating. It helped me get to where I am today. Happier than I have ever been in my life! I've always liked to take the road less traveled. Everyone always tried to put me down for it, for being different. Though, that's what sets people apart. It divides the great people from just the ordinary ones. If you never take risks in your life, you never know what you could accomplish. For instance, for the first time ever in my life, last weekend I actually went up and approached the hottest, tallest, most fit guy in the bar. I normally would have never done this, but I was following my rules and getting out of my comfort zone. He was 6ft 7inches tall and had a rock hard body. I don't even really remember what I said to him, but he turned out to be the nicest guy. He bought my friend and I a drink, we chatted for a while. He told me that everyone thinks he's unapproachable. Girls never come up to him, which is ironic because guys think that I'm unapproachable. We had a great conversation; he was super nice and sweet and at the end of the night asked me for my number and gave me a kiss. Stepping out of my comfort zone really paid off.

Normally I would always date down, go for the guy who I know is a couple rungs lower on the ladder for me because it's a sure win. Though, we can all see how well that's worked out for me in the past. Dating down has put me divorced at 34 with no kids. I have never dated someone that was in my league, someone that made me giddy and warm in fuzzy inside. This 6ft 7inches guy made me melt in my stilettos just being around him. When I looked up at him I completely forgot we were in a bar with hundreds of people around, DJ blaring in the background. Everything tuned out besides he and I. It was the best feeling in the world and also when he went in for the kiss (which I didn't mind at all). I normally don't make out in bars. Yet it wasn't a gross make out drunken session, it was a sweet, simple kiss. Who knows what will become of Mr. 6ft 7inches, but all I know is that now the world is my oyster and anything is possible.

2ND EDITION EXTRA CONTENT

You are one of the lucky ones to have purchased the 2nd edition of "10 Rules to Survive the Dating Jungle" which is full of extra oooey goooey dating goodness! I hope you enjoy the extra information to help you venture back out into the dating jungle. Remember to follow me on social media to have the most up-to-date information as well!

www.facebook.com/datingjungle

www.twitter.com/TaraRRichter

www.twitter.com/datingjungleFL

www.youtube.com/user/DatingJungleBook

www.tampadatingjungle.wordpress.com

www.amazon.com/TaraRichter/e/B00CGKD8FG

5 SIGNS A MAN IS INTO YOU

1) He will start asking questions about you to your friends. Trying to find out more information on who you are. He's intrigued so he will do his research.

2) He will ask you for your number, email, Facebook, business card or any form of contact to stay in touch with you.

3) A man will send you sweet messages like good morning, it was nice meeting you last night etc. to keep the communication alive between you. And because you are obviously on his mind when you are not together.

4) They ask in-depth questions about you, your family, what's your 5 year plan? Your biggest fear? Long term stuff. He is trying to figure out if you have the same life plan and if you would be wife material for him.

5) He will ask you out to do things. If you say no, he'll offer alternative dates and times or leave his schedule open to fit you in. He will make room for you in his life no matter how busy he is. He knows you're special and he doesn't want you to get away.

Signs he's not into you:

He does none of the above. Never ask a man if he wants you're number. If he's interested he will climb mountains, swim through oceans & fight lions to find you.

If a man has your number & doesn't call or text he's either lost interest or isn't ready to pursue things further. He's still processing and testing things out. If a man has time to pee he has time to send you a text message. Give him space, actions speak louder than words.

5 SIGNS YOU'RE DATING THE WRONG PERSON

When you start dating, it takes a while to really get to know someone. Who they are really are, how they handle certain situations, their life's path and if the two of you are compatible or not. What you should do in the beginning is pay close attention to the little things. Actions speak louder than words. Anyone can talk a big talk, but what are the little things they are doing?

1) **How are your conversations?** Do they flow nicely, do you understand each other points of view? Can you have an adult debate without it turning into a boxing match? In the beginning of dating if you feel the person you're dating just doesn't "get" what you are talking about, you probably have different ideologies. Nothing wrong with that, but it's going to make it very difficult to get along with one another. It's going to cause a lot of battles. Especially when you get into a deeper committed relationship.

2) **How does this person make you feel?** Listen to your body & your heart after going on a date with someone. When you leave their presence do you feel light, airy and full of love? Do you have a huge smile on your face that leaves you looking like the Cheshire cat? Or do you feel tired, depleted and negative? If you do not share the same type of

energy they could be zapping yours from you. You need to be with someone who has the same levels of positive energy so you can uplift each other in a healthy way.

3) **Do you have the same life plan?** When you discuss the future are your ideas the same? Do you both want to get married and have kids? Or is one person not sure yet? Would you rather focus on your career and traveling around the world? First of all you need to know what you want prior to dating so you can find someone who wants similar things. If you know 100% you eventually want kids and your BF/GF doesn't, well why waste your time? You're not going to change their mind & if they cave into your demands, eventually down the road they are going to be resentful towards you which is not a good environment for anyone.

4) **Do they treat you with respect?** Do they value your opinions, feedback, morals and listen to you? When you go on dates are you only doing what they want to do? Do you feel like you're always caving in? Or do they have a respect that we'll see a movie I want to tonight and next weekend I'll take you to the sappy chick flick? There has to be a give and take and a mutual respect. There are two people in a relationship, not just one.

5) **Do you have the same belief system when it comes to family?** Meaning have you had the conversation

yet of how you believe a marriage is? People's views are very different but usually very deep rooted in this area. All depending upon their childhood / culture and various aspects. You need to know someone's core belief system. Do you believe in a 50/50 relationship? Or do you want to stay at home and raise kids and the husband is the breadwinner? On the other hand do you want the husband to raise the kids and the woman goes out into the workforce? Or do you think both parents should work fulltime? Who does the chores? Some men think the woman should work and raise the kids and run the household. I don't agree with this philosophy, yet my husband did. This is why he is now my ex-husband. We didn't discuss prior to marriage, well I told him what I believed and he sat quietly thinking he could change me once we were married. That is a HUGE mistake. You will not change anyone. Accept them for who they are and have open and honest discussions both of your belief systems.

The key here is COMMUNICATION. You have to have OPEN HONEST COMMUNICATION. You cannot just listen and make your own assumptions about a person. People may only talk about certain topics because that's what's going on in their life at that particular time. Just because a woman is passionate about her business and she talks about it a lot is because that's the main focus in life at that time. It doesn't mean that she doesn't want kids and a family in the future. It means she doesn't have that in her life at that time. It also doesn't mean that she doesn't know how to balance work, kids and a husband. She will do that when all those aspects are in her life.

Don't judge, ask questions. Have open non-pressure conversations to find out. Say something like, "I'm just curious, so I see you are very passionate about your work, yet how would you fit a family in there?" Women are amazing human beings we are super woman. We can work 3 jobs, raise children, clean the house, make a fantastic dinner and still be a sex goddess. However the balance comes when the husband and wife work together to make harmony in each other's life.

So when you start dating, have those small non-pressure conversations. "I'm just wondering…." Find out before you get too deeply involved. It will save you a lot of heartache.

HOW TO GET A DATE IN 20 MINS OR LESS

Getting dates is really easier than you think. I was going to a black tie event in Tampa Bay and I wanted a date to accompany me. I had a few guys I know would go, but I wanted to take someone new. So I posted an AD on Craigslist (yes Craigslist) for exactly what I was looking for and got my date in less than 20 minutes.

1) **Be precise for what you are looking for.** I knew exactly what "type" of guy I wanted to attend the event with me. I want him to look good in a suite or tux, tall, attractive and be able to carry on an intelligent conversation. Since this event is going to be filled with business owners, I needed to know he could rub elbows with that sort of crowd. So I titled my AD, "Seeking Gentlemen to be my date for a Black Tie Event." By doing this I weeded out the men that wouldn't wear a tux or be comfortable in that environment.

2) **Within the AD describe in more detail.** Then I spelled it out that you have to be intelligent, I wanted someone tall because I am tall and when wearing heels I don't want to tower over my date. I also put my age to hopefully get men in my dating pool (no more than 10 years older of younger.)

3) **Post a good photo of you.** I put a photo of myself from New Year's Eve dress up. So they would see

what I look like in fancy attire. Make sure to take an excellent photo of yourself and put your best foot forward. Even if you have a few pounds to lose, wear an outfit that compliments your figure. Stand in a way that the camera and angles show you in the best light. You can take off 20 pounds with the right techniques. I teach all my girlfriends this move. Stand tall and straight, then take your left foot out and point it. Say if your facing N your left foot would be pointing W. You twist your body, your hips are point E & W then twist your shoulders towards N & S. Twisting, sucking in, chin out & voilà! You've lost 20 pounds & elongated your body & will look great in photos.

4) **Weed Out Responses Quickly.** After posting my AD I received about 50 emails in less than 20 minutes. I had to take it down soon after because my email box was flooded with men. Since I was very precise in what I was looking for I had guys emailing me photos of themselves in suits & tuxedos! It was fantastic I didn't even have to leave my house while I did the casting call. I quickly scanned the photos & what they wrote. I had non-negotiables in mind & weeded out the ones that didn't fit. The 7th email I read was exactly what I wanted: 33 years old, 6 ft tall, curly brown hair, pretty eyes, has written & published a book of his own (awesome I know we are similar in that regard) he designs websites (I have a degree in graphic design) & he's originally

from Wisconsin, perfect I'm from the Midwest too! He also looked good in his suit, winner winner chicken dinner! I found my date in less than 20 minutes! I emailed him & we set up a meeting for coffee the following day.

Bonus was he showed up in a '77 Mustang Fastback, one of my favorite cars! And looked just like his photos. If you're not getting the responses you want, it might be your photos, your headline or you're not describing in detail exactly what you want. Be honest with yourself how are people really seeing you? Are you representing yourself honestly? Do you need to lose some weight? Get your hair done. Yes, people can criticize and say I get a date in 20 minutes because I'm good looking, well let me tell you I didn't always look like this.

In high-school I was overweight, nerdy & played the cello. Do you think I got dates then? Absolutely not. I was unhappy with myself so I changed. Over the course of a summer I lost weight figured out how to dress and do my hair & makeup from watching movies & reading magazines. I went from orchestra nerd to being voted most desirable female of the senior class. It can be done! I did it myself. I can help you too. If you think you're in need of a dating make-over contact me today & find out about my Dating Jungle Boot Camp!

HOW SHOULD YOU BREAK UP?

I was on the Josh Tolley Radio Show and we were discussing how to heal a broken heart. As Josh stated the broken heart is usually because of the way the relationship ended, which is very true. If we had better communication skills and treated others, especially our partners, with love and respect there would be less heartache. He suggested I write about how people should break up. I think it's a great topic. I have briefly touched on it in the past, but I think it's an issue worth revisiting.

When you decide the person you have been dating, in a relationship with or married to for however many years, just isn't working, you owe it to them to have an open honest conversation. You should start talking about it as soon as you are having feelings of uncertainty. Of course most people don't. They instead talk about it with their friends, family or co-workers. When you venture outside of the relationship for emotional support, in a way, you are emotionally cheating on your partner.

You should be able to share your feelings openly and freely with your lover. They are supposed to be with you through thick and thin. If they won't listen to your feelings or refuse to communicate with you, this could be a reason why you are thinking of breaking up.

However, if you haven't even tried to talk about your concerns, start their first and see what happens.

Many times when we are going through problems in our heads we make them out to be something bigger than what it really is. Once we talk about it with the person we are having the issue, it may completely diffuse itself and save your relationship. Give your partner the chance to at least know what's going on inside you. Keep them in the loop.

If that still doesn't work and you do want to end the relationship, be honest with them as to why. Don't just pack up your stuff and leave in the middle of the night; for them to wake up clueless as to what happened. Then they are left holding a broken heart and a bag of questions. Why? What happened? What did I do wrong? Why me?

Be an adult and have that difficult conversation, it will save a whole lot of drama down the road. Even if it was someone who you only dated for a few months. If you decided they are just not the one for you, don't vanish to the island of lost men and avoid their phone calls and text messages. Be a man, answer their questions. When people leave lovers high and dry with no explanation, that's when perfectly normal men and women go psychotic. Cars get keyed, clothes thrown on the lawn, or someone may put on adult diapers an drive across country to find you.

This momentary lapse in judgment is because the person doing the severing of the relationship without communication is tapping into your rejection and abandonment issues that are deep seeded inside your subconscious mind. Every time that you have ever been rejected bubbles up to the surface. All your issues: from that one time mom left you at kindergarten all alone by accident, your father leaving the family due to divorce, to your first boyfriend or girlfriend dumping you, etc. So it's no wonder people go crazy.

Your inner child is feeling hurt and sad, so you act out to defend yourself and your ego. A fight or flight response to protect yourself from more harm. If instead the person leaving sat you down and had a heart-to-heart conversation so you could understand their feelings and you both could communicate openly, it would go much smoother. In fact you could still be friends and not have to dodge each other's favorite hang outs. Yes, feelings may still be hurt, but at least you gave them an opportunity to have a say in the matter.

Just remember to treat others with love and respect and they most likely will do the same in return.

HOW TO GET A MAN TO APPROACH YOU

When you are out and about in the dating jungle as a woman, you want to make yourself approachable. Believe it or not, men do have a hard time approaching women. Even when they are successful & intelligent human beings, because no one likes rejection. Many times the shy ones are the good guys. Have you ever had the feeling that you only attract the douche bags? How come I never like any of the men that like me?

If you've ever had that feeling, try this trick. When you are out and about with your girlfriends, separate yourself from the crowd. Men have a hard time approaching a group of women. It's hard enough to possibly get rejected from one girl let alone being embarrassed in front of a group of them. It's much easier to talk a woman who is by herself.

Instead of going to the bathroom in a group, like us women normally do, hang back and "save the table" for everyone. Show up to dinner with your girlfriend early and hang out at the bar and have a glass of wine while you wait for her. I can guarantee if there's a man interested in you in that room, he will make a move while you are alone.

It took me even awhile to see this pattern happening to myself. I was out with my girlfriend over Memorial Day weekend at Blue Martini in Fort Lauderdale. The place was packed, we sat at a high-top table and I saw a few guys checking me out. They circled around the table looking over, but scared to do anything. As soon as my friend went over to the bar to get us a drink, one of them swooped in and sat next to me. Then another walked by and gave him a dirty look as if to say, damn you got there first. It was hilarious. Then after he left sometime later and my girlfriend left again to go to the bathroom another one swooped in and took her spot.

It finally clicked in my head. These guys will not approach me unless I'm alone because it's easier on them. I have no idea why I never got this conception my twenties, yet I possibly wasn't paying attention. I was also tight in my pack of girlfriends making myself very unapproachable. Remember to smile and make yourself inviting too, obviously sitting alone with a scowl on your face isn't going to invite anyone to join you no matter how long you're sitting alone. They probably figure there's a reason why no one's sitting next to you.

When you are sitting there by yourself for however long, don't pick up your smart phone and become engulfed in Facebook land. I know I'm guilty of this as well. It seems in this day and age if we are alone for a mere few seconds, we have this knee jerk response to get lost in the digital world. How easy would it be for a stranger to talk to you then? Think about it, would go up and talk to someone who is looking down reading their phone? No, you probably wouldn't. Because you would feel like you're bothering them. So pull yourself off your iPhone and get back to the real world that's happening to you right now right in front of you. Smile, make eye contact with a guy walking by. Just that simple gesture can open conversation and break the ice to meet new and interesting people.

THROW THE MAN A BONE

By this I don't mean treat them like a dog, even though some guys deserve it, not all guys, but yes some are dogs. I'm talking about something different.

When you're out with your girlfriends at a bar or nightclub and you see the guy across the way that keeps starring at you, yet won't come over and make the first move. You've given him all the signals, flipping the hair, direct eye contact and flirting. Yet he's still nervous. He may even be standing right next to you, starring at you but won't say anything.

This man may be intimidated, shy or not used to approaching a strong woman. There are the small majority of men that will approach a confidant woman without any signals from her at all. He just goes all in because he wants to talk to her and he has the self-esteem to do so. Other men need a little reassurance before making the plunge into uncharted territory.

So lately I have been practicing what I like to call "Throw the man a bone." If I'm out somewhere and I see a man checking me out more than a few times, and he has not made the move, I will throw him a bone. I do this by asking him something. Such as I was out at Blue Martini in Fort Lauderdale the other weekend and my girlfriend and I were up at the bar ordering a drink. The guy standing next to me looked like a taller bigger version of Vin Diesel. He kept looking at me, but wouldn't say anything. There was an awesome electronic violist playing up behind the bar and I leaned over to the guy and said, "This guy is pretty cool, does he play here often? I'm from Tampa so I haven't been here before." I threw out the bone.

It was enough for him to open communication and start a discussion. Sometimes even if a guy thinks you are attractive they are scared to initiate contact, even when you have given them the nonverbal cues it's ok to do so. Some men do not pick up on this. The male editor of my first book loved my last two chapters when I discussed the art of flirting. He put it in the note section, "I wish I would have read this book 10 years ago before I was married. I had no idea women were flirting with me back when I was dating."

Women give men the non-verbal come hither signs. Yet many of the men do not pick up on them. Then you have the douche bags that come over and kiss you on the face without your permission. It's the good guys that misinterpret our signals or maybe take too long to pick up on them. Then you're stuck on the dance floor with sweaty, gross guy who won't take his hands off your ass.

If you see a guy who you think might be worth talking to more and he keeps checking you out, throw him a bone and see if he takes the bait. Once you open the lines of communication you never know where the night might lead.

HOW TO NOT SNATCH A SUCCESSFUL MAN

During a great networking event in Tampa one night, I witnessed a woman doing everything wrong in the dating jungle. After an all day workshop learning from leaders in the industry there was an after party in Ybor. Alcoholic beverages were flowing and articulate conversations were dancing on intellectual tongues. I heard in the distance a man mention my radio show, so I went over to join the conversation. Two minutes later, the woman he was discussing it with, blurted out to me that she wanted to take him home and bang his brains out. He and I immediately turned to one another with a look of Scooby Doo, "Huh."

If she was looking for shock factor she definitely achieved it. However, I don't think that's what she was going for. I immediately responded with, "Dating Coach says NO!" She responded that she needed to get laid, it's been a year & a half because she's going through a divorce.

This is a pure example of why you need to take time off to heal your wounds while you're going through a difficult divorce/ break up. Otherwise you'll have one too many cocktails at a networking event and end up humping a dating coach's leg. (Yes, that happened that night as well. Good thing most of the people had already left the bar.)

She's a hot mess. I know because I have been in her shoes before. I was a hot mess during & about six months after my divorce. I tried to date & I realized I was nowhere near being emotionally ready for a relationship. So I quit going out to bars trying to drown my sorrows in martinis & men. I instead focused on writing my books, healing my wounds & making rules for myself to stick to. I like structure & I think when you're going through an emotional difficult time, structure is good to follow. It gives you something of purpose that tells you what to do during an upheaval of your life. Having something solid to hold onto can help you know that there is a light at the end of a tunnel.

Now many people protest with me that their divorce has taken a year and a half to finalize, they're healed & ready to move on. I say take another year off once you get the final piece of paper from the judge, because that's another huge emotional slap in the face. You are going to need time to recover from that as well. In the long run, what's another year to better you in the scope of an entire life span of 90 years? This woman also protested with me that she was healed. Does going up to a world renown speaker at a high status networking event & telling him (and to everyone for that matter) that she wants to bang his brains out, then humping my leg sound like she's emotionally sound to date? Dating Coach says no.

With that being said once she is ready to date, snatching up a successful business man is a fine art. You can't just lay the platter out for him right in front of his face. These men are creatures who have busted their butts and overcome most odds to be in a highly respected place. They love to overcome all obstacles, it's in their DNA.

An easy woman who places no challenge to him is boring. He wants someone to push him mentally, physically, emotionally & spiritually. Yes, dating is partially a game & you need to know how to play it. Think of men as different levels of card games. Some card games are simple and require no skill, such as War or 52 card pick up. Then there are mid-level games with some skill like 21. Subsequently there are top level poker tournaments that require high level strategy. These types of events would not allow 52 card pick up to participate in the competition because there's no skill to it. If you want to be with a top poker champion, you have to learn how to play their game. Don't be the woman with all her cards showing on the floor at once. Play the game. Place bets even if you don't have a Royal Flush in your hands, because it will make him want to raise the stakes and think you are worth staying in the game for.

DON'T RE-DATE YOUR EX

If you broke up with somebody, you broke up for a purpose. Don't try to re-kindle something did not work out in the past. It didn't work out for a reason. Sometimes people come in and out of our lives for an objective, a lesson to be learned. It can be a long lesson like marriage or a short one like a boyfriend. Whatever reasons you broke up with that person for are going to bubble again in a second attempt. Save both yourselves the trouble and move on.

It's hard after you've spent time apart because you forget the entire "thing" that drove you crazy when you were together. They start to fade away along with the memories. Then you run into them at a bar our out with friends a few years later, strike up conversation and think to yourself, "Why did we break up again?"

TRUST ME — *IT HAPPENED FOR A REASON.*

People are in our lives for a purpose and people leave our lives for a purpose. If you force the issue the result is usually not enjoyable. Events in life should happen organically. If you're pushing or pulling too hard to get back together with someone, then it's the universes way of saying stop, this is not what's meant for you. Take a step back, breathe deeply, and be patient. Whatever is meant for you will happen in due time.

Remember, the more time you spend with Mr. / Mrs. Past it leaves you less time to find Mr. / Mrs. Perfect For You. You deserve to be with someone that's going to give you a loving lasting relationship. There are over 6 billion some people on the planet. I'm sure you can find someone better than your ex.

BE THE WOMAN THAT MAKES MEN SWOON

Men can smell a desperate woman a mile away. Those males who want to take advantage of an easy to manipulate and control female will be attracted to them like a magnet. They can hunt them out of a crowd like a jaguar hunting its prey. They can sense on a subconscious level this type of woman will not put up much of a fight and it's an easy kill. Insecure women with low self-esteem demonstrate these qualities without even knowing it. Like an invisible aura around you. That aura attracts the type of mate who within himself is also insecure deep down inside.

However, the same is true for a strong, emotionally stable, happy, independent woman. The insecure male who goes after desperate women, will be scared away by such strength because he knows deep down inside this type of woman will call him out on his shit and won't put up with it. He knows that men can come and go out of her life and she will be just fine. Why? Because her self-worth comes within and not from a man. A real man will also sense this on a subconscious level and be attracted to her. The kind of man she needs who is also strong and confident.

A real man who's resilient, self-assured, loving and sincere will be bored with the clingy, desperate women. Its way to easy for him and he will bull doze them over.

Not even because he wants to, but because it's in his nature. He needs and wants a woman who challenges him mentally, physically and will call him out when he's wrong. But will also support, love and stand by him forever. This real man doesn't want a "yes" woman he wants someone who will tell him the truth. "Yes" people don't help us grow and develop. Only the truth does. If you're confident within yourself you can be honest and tell the truth to a man. He will love you for it.

Be that strong, confident woman that men swoon too and can't get enough of. How can you achieve this? By loving you and making a full, rich life for yourself independent of a man. So when the total package comes into your life, he'll want to share in the happiness you've made. He will sense deep down inside that your self-esteem doesn't depend on him. That you don't need him to survive, you want him to take part in your wonderful life. That will be a relief to him since so many women do the opposite. When he doesn't have all the pressure of your life riding on him day to day, he can relax and be himself around you, which is what he ultimately desires to do. Then both of you can just have fun and enjoy each other's company and allow true love to develop.

IS THE GRASS GREENER ON THE OTHER SIDE?

We all know this old saying, yet people have different opinions on it. Some say the grass is always greener on the other side meaning that you are always chasing after something bigger and better and you're never happy with what you have. Other people disagree and state that the grass is never greener on the other side. We should learn to live with what we have and deal with it.

In terms of dating sometimes the grass might be greener on the other side, yet you have to know when to hop over the fence and take that chance. Especially if you are in a current committed relationship. You have to do what's right and end your relationship before testing out a new one. If you haven't already had the exclusive talk, then you need to assume both parties are still dating around. However, if you did agree to only see each other, do the right thing & end it. If someone else grabs your attention & you want to test out the new lawn, you can't fully until you're uncommitted. It's not fair to either party to try to start a new relationship with one foot still in the old one. It's impossible to completely give yourself to the other person & they can sense it.

Additionally, if you were copiously in love with the first person then the second person wouldn't have been able to pull your focus away. Sometimes in life a better person does come along, yet you have to do the right thing. If you really want to explore a new relationship you must end your current one, be honest, open as to why & be able to reap the consequences of your actions. The newer relationship may not work & your old flame may not ever take you back, but doing the right thing for you will feel good when you're honest with all parties involved. If you don't end the current relationship & try to test out the waters with the new person, that's called cheating & no one likes a cheater. Feelings will get hurt; bigger messes will get made that you can't clean up because you were trying to protect your heart by not fully giving it to one or the other person.

Sometimes you have to live life on a whim & a prayer by putting yourself out there 100%. Open yourself up to possible failure/ rejection or hopefully everlasting true love. People who live life always protecting their hearts will never experience the joys of finding that "can't live without you" love. You have to take big risks in life to harvest great rewards.

As author Robert Fulghum stated, "The grass is not, in fact, always greener on the other side of the fence. No, not at all. Fences have nothing to do with it. The grass is greenest where it is watered. When crossing over fences, carry water with you and tend the grass wherever you are."

OPEN YOUR HEART

When you're dating someone in the beginning stages watch for signs that this is the one for you. The signs I of speak of are within our feelings. Emotions that bubble up deep inside you caused by being around or thinking if this special person. Sometimes we got so caught up of over analyzing every aspect of this person, a "good on paper" type of review, we forget to how to feel.

Remember your very first crush? Do you remember the first time you fell in love? Recall back in middle or high school when the boy you liked said hi passing you by in the hallways? You blushed, pulling your books up to cover your sheepish grin and it felt like it was only the two of you in the entire school because time stopped and everyone else faded into the background? That's the feeling I'm talking about!

We need to get back to listening to our feelings and stop over analyzing everything. Yes, you want to make rational decisions, but hold out for the one that makes you giddy inside, gives you butterflies, makes you glow just thinking or talking about them. After going through bitter break-ups and bad divorces we get jaded, scorned and put our walls up. We don't want to let someone in 100% again because we are so terrified of putting our hearts on our sleeves. Ironically though, that's the only way you can find true love. If you never put yourself out on a hope and a whim how will anyone else ever do the same for you?

That's why it's so important to heal your wounds like I talk about in both of my books. Without healing yourself you will never be able to fully love again with an open heart. People will be able to sense your walls. Who wants to be an old, alone & cynical at 70? I don't think any of us do, but it happens, to a lot of people. I'm sure you've encountered many of these people I'm speaking of. Don't let yourself become one!

Let your heart open to new experiences and new people. Hold out for the person that makes you as excited & silly like a high school crush. You can't wait for their phone call, to see them again and be in their presence. Someone that makes you want to listen to those sappy love songs on the radio. Who makes you want to be a better person. When you look into their eyes everyone else disappears and it feels like time stops. It may take years but you will eventually find that person. A friend of mine who I interviewed for my "10 Rules to Survive the Internet Dating Jungle" found his angle on Match.com; after being married divorced and searching for her for 18 years. They are now in their 60s, but he finally found her. Wouldn't you rather wait for "can't live without you love" versus settling for "it's just ok love"?

If the person you are dating doesn't give you butterflies, doesn't make you want to go to the mountain tops and scream it to everyone that you're so happy to have found this person, then they may not be the one for you. If you don't have those intense feelings in the beginning you probably never will. Usually feelings are going to settle down, after the initial honeymoon phases, so if you're not having it now it's not going to suddenly pop up six months from now. Everyone deserves to have a partner who's completely and utterly in love with them, and you with them. Don't settle for less.

WHEN SHOULD YOU HAVE THE EXCLUSIVE TALK?

When you first start dating someone, it really doesn't really matter who initiates the conversation of becoming exclusive. You should definitely have the monogamy talk either before having sex with your partner or shortly thereafter. There is really no time frame of when you should have the talk. But more or less when you feel comfortable and you know that you don't want to date anyone else. Definitely not after the first date because that's too soon and way creepy. Then it depends on how often you are seeing each other. Are you only going on one date every other week, one date a month, or do you see the person two – three times a week?

You want to make sure that you do bring up the conversation of being monogamous especially after having sex with your significant other. You don't want to assume exclusivity, though sometimes as women we do. That's a mistake, just because you have sex doesn't mean the other person is going to commit to you. In every relationship you have to accept that everyone is dating other people until you have that exclusivity conversation. You have to bring it up in person so you know that both of you are on the same page and there's no confusion. If you avoid the uncomfortable conversation your feelings and heart can be broken if you just assume you are monogamous and then find out that your partner isn't. But without the conversation you're assuming your partner is able to read your mind, in reality they cannot, so really you only have yourself to blame.

However, having the exclusive talk should not be uncomfortable with the right person. If during the conversation you feel uneasy and unsure of yourself, it could be that the person you're having it with is reluctant to be exclusive with you. At that point you should wonder why you want to be relationship with somebody who does not want to be in one with you? You deserve to be with someone who wants to make you their center of attention and does not want to share their love with anyone else. If you've spent a lot of time with this person, having sexual relations and they still do not want to see you exclusively; you should dump them, move on and find someone who will.

RELAX AND HAVE FUN ON DATES!

Remember when you are out in the dating jungle to relax and have fun! Don't put too much pressure on the situation. Going out on a first meeting, have the mindset that "I'm going to meet a new friend today!" instead of "I'm meeting my future wife/ husband."

I was discussing the concept with one of my girlfriends. And she put it so eloquently, "When I date a guy for however long, I just enjoy the time we have together. I have no expectations for how long it will last. If we spend a month together and then it's over, well I had a great time during that month and then it's time to move on."

I think this is a great philosophy to live by. Because for one people come and go out of our lives for a reason and lesson to be learned. Sometimes they are short lessons and sometimes lifelong lessons. Instead of gripping and holding onto someone to full-fill your dreams, live in the moment. Enjoy that person for who they are & what kind of joy they bring to your life for whatever duration of time.

Stop placing so many high expectations on situations. And placing your happiness within someone else. Only you can truly bring happiness into your life. Just go out there and have some fun. If things lead to a long term commitment or marriage then so be it, but don't force it. concentrate on you and what makes you happy. Once you're happy other inspirational people will be drawn into your life.

ABOUT THE AUTHOR

Tara Richter is an author, publisher & writing coach. She specializes in coaching people how to write their non-fiction story in 4 weeks & publish a book. She has been featured on CNN, ABC, Daytime Tv, Fox, SSN, Channel 10 News, USA Today & Beverly Hills Times.

Her degree is in graphic design and she worked in the copy and print industry in the silicon valley. She has written and published 12 of her own books in just a few short years. Tara now has published many authors in her local Tampa bay area including Anthony Amos & celebrity entrepreneur, Kevin Harrington, shark from ABC'S "Shark Tank" with their joint book, "How To Catch A Shark."

She has streamlined the complex writing and publishing industry so anyone can become a published author in just a few weeks! Visit her website:

www.richterpublishing.com

Awards:

2013 Finalist For Tampa Bay's Business Woman Of The Year Award
2014 Nominee For Tampa's Up & Coming Businesses
2015 Nominee For 2015 Iconic Woman Of The Year
2015 Finalist For Best In Biz From Local Shops 1
2015 Amazon Best Selling Author & Hot New Release
2016 Recipient Of H.E.R.O. Award From Fulfill Your Destiny
2017 Commencement Speaker For Keiser University Graduation
2019 Nominee for Tampa Bay's Corporate Philanthropy Award

10 RULES TO SURVIVE THE DATING JUNGLE

www.ingramcontent.com/pod-product-compliance
Lightning Source LLC
Chambersburg PA
CBHW051835090426
42736CB00011B/1818